Issues in Education
GENERAL EDITOR: PHILIP HILLS

The Education of the Whole Child

D1405831

Other books in this series

Michael Barber: *Education and the Teacher Unions*

Gordon Batho: *Political Issues in Education*

David Bosworth: *Open Learning*

Janet Collins: *The Quiet Child*

John Darling and Anthony Glendinning: *Gender Matters in Schools*

Norman Evans: *Experiential Learning for All*

Paul Fisher: *Education 2000*

Leo Hendry, Janet Shucksmith and Kate Philip: *Educating for Health*

Eric Hoyle and Peter John: *Professional Knowledge and Professional Practice*

Roy Todd: *Education in a Multicultural Society*

Geoffrey Walford: *Choice and Equity in Education*

Michael Williams: *In-service Education and Training*

Forthcoming:

Nicholas Gair: *The Theory and Practice of Outdoor Education*

David Sanders and Leo Hendry: *New Perspectives on Disaffection*

The authors would like to thank the children and teachers who have generously helped us with this research. Without their trust and respect we could not have done this work.

Acknowledgements

Extracts from 'Ithaca' (on p. 14) from *The Complete Poems of C.P. Cavafy,* translated by Rae Dalven, are reproduced by permission of Random House UK Limited.

Extract from 'Little Gidding' (p. 180) from *Four Quartets* is reproduced by permission of Faber and Faber Ltd.

'Looking for Dad' (on pp. 45–6), copyright © Brian Patten 1985, and 'The Minister for Exams' (on pp. 135–6), copyright © Brian Patten 1996, are reproduced by permission of the author, c/o Rogers, Coleridge and White Ltd, 20 Powis Mews, London W11 1JN.

Foreword: The purpose of this series

The educational scene is changing rapidly. This change is being caused by a complexity of factors which includes a re-examination of present educational provision against a background of changing social and economic policies, the 1988 Education Reform Act, new forms of testing and assessment, a National Curriculum, and local management of schools with more participation by parents.

As the educational process is concerned with every aspect of our lives and our society both now and for the future, it is of vital importance that all teachers, teachers in training, administrators and educational policy-makers should be aware and informed on current issues in education.

This series of books is thus designed to inform on current issues, look at emerging ones, and to give an authoritative overview which will be of immense help to all those involved in the education process.

Philip Hills
Cambridge

Introduction

In her book *I Answer with My Life: Life Histories of Women Teachers Working for Social Change,* Kathleen Casey explains how she uses the linguistic theories of Mikhail Bakhtin as a basis for the analysis of her data. She says:

> The most important contribution of Bakhtin's theories, from my point of view, is the way in which they make possible the combination of a serious intellectual analysis of women teachers' narratives with a profound respect for their authors.

This attitude to the research which she carried out resonates for us with the work that we have done with children. We started the project that resulted in this book partly because we were sure that children's needs were not being catered for in the education system of this country on account of their opinions not being sought or acted upon.

The Children and Worldviews Project was set up as a collaborative venture, funded by three colleges of higher education: Chichester Institute, King Alfred's College, Winchester, and La Sainte Union College, Southampton. The founder members were all lecturers in education at these colleges: Clive Erricker at Chichester, Danny Sullivan at LSU and Jane Erricker at King Alfred's. A research assistant, Cathy Ota, joined us to work for her PhD and help develop the Project's research. The project has been researching for the last three years, giving papers at conferences and publishing articles arising from our research in schools.

This book represents a report of the work carried out so far. It is divided into three sections. Section One sets the context for the research in terms of the present educational climate in which it took place. Section Two tells the stories of the research done by various members of the team. Section Three outlines the implications of the research as we see them, with regard to educational policy and provision and strategies for the classroom.

The style of the research is one which acknowledges the subjectivity of the researcher, allowing him or her to bring their intuition and personal involvement to the research situation. As this attitude is freely admitted and justified in the section on methodology, we felt it appropriate to write in the first person and to attribute each chapter to the particular person(s) who carried out the research.

Our hope is that this work will inform teachers and others involved in educational policy and management as to what children can bring to this venture, which is often not recognized. We believe, also, that such recognition should have a substantial influence on educational debate.

Section One

The context of the research

development devolves from the top down and the outcome is perceived as already determined. Content is the key concern. This approach is insufficient not simply because it can be criticized ideologically, for example, because not all children will be or will wish to be Christian, but because it fundamentally ignores the developmental issues involved.

Our second example relates more closely to Plutarch's view. It comes from the 'Face to Faith' column in the *Guardian* and was written by Don Cupitt on the same day as the previous one under the title 'What's the Big Idea'.

Knowledge realized

In the past, the moral order and the religious order looked very much more secure and objective than they do today. The right answers to all the big questions were already known, being embodied in and taught by our established social and religious institutions. Ideas were not really necessary, and critical thinking was not necessary. It was sufficient to instruct the young in the established orthodoxy, A century later, we no longer have any such consensus. Yet we still cling to the vestiges of the old conviction that the system already knows all the answers. In our schools we are instructed to teach current scientific theory in a largely unhistorical and uncritical way, and chiefly with a view to preparing people to operate the new technologies. We teach novels, plays and poems as 'literature', having largely cut the thinkers out of the literary canon. We teach religion and morality positively, rather than teaching children how to assess the rationality of the varied beliefs and values they will be meeting in the world outside school ... We give the impression of being more concerned about training than education. So the Big Idea is ideas. We need democratic philosophy. It is true, unfortunately, that the churches will promptly stamp on any attempt to make their teachings more rational; but whatever they say, we need and we must teach a new and genuinely independent style of critical religious thought. We've got to restart morality. And all this needs to be done, not just by and for a handful of intellectuals, but at the democratic and popular level. In schools.

And politics has got to be about more than just managing the economy and training people to be technicians in the daytime and couch potatoes in the evening.   (*Guardian, 29* June 1995)

Cupitt's polemic represents a point of view that has been espoused ever since the Enlightenment, and the two passages act together as footnotes to the debate that began at that time and is still not resolved. It is central to the concerns of education. The accent of Cupitt's argument is that education should not be a handmaiden to a particular ideological position, which he identifies as religious, but should be based upon democratic principles that are the expression of individuals acting in a social group. This possibility depends on our educational system acquainting children with the world of ideas and encouraging them to be thinkers in their own right. The result of this would be a society which is politically alive, rationally competent and open to change and plurality of view. Though idealistic in his tone, Cupitt does address educational issues concerning development in a way that the previous writer does not, and in this sense aligns himself with the notions of process education and progressive theories influential in the 1960s and 1970s.

Underpinning Cupitt's view and those of other educational theorists consonant with his is the idea that education has an open-ended outcome which will radically affect the society in which it takes place. This is based on the processes of communication, negotiation, reflection and rational thinking which in turn will produce change. Implicit in this, though not overtly stated, is the presumption that change will lead to progress because it is based on the right principles. What Cupitt does not address is how far rationality can be taken as an objective and sufficient principle for the educational process and the development of the child. Here his argument is subject to the same criticisms that have been traditionally directed at Enlightenment thinkers. The dispute outlined above is at the centre of our theories of knowledge and fundamentally affects our vision of education and the construction of the curriculum. This is the case because knowledge is related to truth and the means by which we arrive at knowing what is true. If truth is 'God-given' and therefore absolute and unchanging, it must be handed down. If what is true is arrived at by rational exploration, then it may change in a progressive fashion in accordance with the development of enquiry.

The role of narrative

Neither of the above approaches, however, takes account of a third factor, which is that truth may be related to personal narrative constructed out of individual experience. It is this element that we will now discuss. This is a contentious topic because it implicitly questions whether either of the above positions may be a preferred starting point for our educational endeavour. Barbara Hardy, in a chapter entitled 'Narrative as a primary act of mind' in *The Cool Web* (Meek *et al.*, 1977), comments on the role of story-telling in relation to the construction of meaning and order in our experiences.

> I take for granted the ways in which storytelling engages our interest, curiosity, fear, tensions, expectation, and sense of order. What concerns me here are the qualities which fictional narrative shares with that inner and outer storytelling that plays a major role in our sleeping and waking lives. For we dream in narrative, daydream in narrative, remember, anticipate, hope, despair, believe, doubt, plan, revise, criticise, construct, gossip, learn, hate and love by narrative. In order really to live, we make up stories about ourselves and others, about personal as well as the social past and future.

Hardy's comments raise important questions regarding the principles on which we base our task as teachers. If we accept that children already possess a narrative within which they construct meaning, then it is meaning rather than truth or knowledge that underpins the education of the whole child. To put this simply, we cannot impose a narrative upon them which does not engage with their own, nor a rationality which does not make sense in terms of the way they have constructed meaning from their experiences. This makes the task of educating children much more provisional and tentative. It is contextualized by the relationships that we develop with the children in our care and has to acknowledge that their reality is the starting point for our communication with them. It also determines the way in which we should understand the child's development. As Gordon Wells writes in *The Meaning Makers* (1986):

> We are the meaning makers – every one of us: children, parents, and teachers. To try to make sense, to construct stories, and to share them with others in speech and in writing is an essential part of being human. For those of us who are more knowledgeable and more mature – parents and teachers – the responsibility is clear: to interact with those in our care in such a way as to foster and enrich *their* meaning making. (Wells, 1986, p. 22)

The implications involved in this are twofold: (1) It presumes that affective learning is at the heart of education. This means that emotions and imagination are as significant as the intellect and tradition; and (2) that individual storying is the basis on which notions of reality are constructed. This is not to disavow the importance of enculturation or instruction. These are both significant elements in the process of learning, but they cannot be addressed in a vacuum independent of engaging with the evolving worldviews of children, which are the outcome of their own narratives.

Michel Foucault wrote: 'What matters is to create the conditions whereby we can all be artists of our own lives.' The choice of the word 'artist' is highly significant since to regard a child as such influences the relationship we have with that child. We must take account of the different facets that constitute the creation of his or her whole identity. As a first step on this path we might invoke the four principles that Wells suggests apply to our communication with children.

- To treat what the child has to say as worthy of careful attention.
- To do one's best to understand what he or she means.
- To take the child's meaning as a basis for what one says next.
- In selecting and encoding one's message, to take account of the

child's ability to understand – that is, to construct an appropriate interpretation.

Engaging with children's minds

In order to undertake this task effectively we must recognize a principle of 'intersubjectivity' that defines our relationship with the child and contextualizes their learning. It is not enough to think of ourselves as conveying objective truths or factual knowledge as the basis of our professional task. The implications of this involve appreciating how the learner perceives him or herself and how that perception influences what goes on in the classroom. Both the teacher and the child are engaged in the exploration of the child's mind, in a rational and affective sense. Our minds can be compared to landscapes within which we map our world and the relationships from which it is constructed. To make sense of this idea we can adapt an observation made by the anthropologist Sheila Kitzinger.

> A condition known as kayak-angst has been described among Eskimos. When the Eskimo hunter is out alone on a calm sea paddling or sitting quietly, there develops a lowering in the level of consciousness brought on by the absence of external reference points at a time when the hunter is engaged in simple repetitive movements or sitting motionless and staring at the sea. He gets confused and dizzy – and even the psychologists who were studying this found that they were disturbed in exactly the same way when they tried to do it too. (Kitzinger, 1987, pp. 184–5)

Kitzinger's observations work on a metaphoric as well as a literal level. Disorientation generally, as well as in the above instance, is a result of being unable to relate to the familiar structure of our world. The absence of a landscape or of those close to us is not merely a case of sensory deprivation but of psychic disorientation. In these cases the world around us when experienced in a sensory manner bears no relation to that which we regard as important or meaningful in our lives. The psychologist William James has referred to this in

11

commenting on the way our thoughts relate to our experiences by suggesting that a satisfactory or balanced state of mind is only attained when one's conceptual and immediately experienced worlds form a consistent and harmonious whole. We may regard the environment to which Kitzinger refers as being the relationship between our immediate sensory experience and the world of our psyche. The capacity to live well or positively depends on this metaphorical reality and its adequacy. We may refer to this as the child's worldview, made up of many stories which give it meaning. To the extent to which this mental landscape is denied or eroded by the immediate physical or social environment that we find ourselves in, so we become disabled in an emotional, intellectual, moral and spiritual way. This amounts to a condition of alienation and it is precisely what we are capable of inflicting on children if we deny them the capacity to affirm and to construct and develop their own metaphorical landscape.

We can illustrate something of this process with reference to a 7-year-old girl, P, whose grandfather died shortly after she was born. He had met her in the first two weeks of her life but she of course could not remember him. In family conversations, stories about him were told by her older brother and sister and parents. He was part of their world but excluded from hers. As a result, in trying to rectify this situation, she would ask what had happened to him and where she could find his grave. He was cremated and there was no place to go where she could find evidence of him having lived. There was no concrete way, whether via memorial or memory, by which she could share in his life. In a small way this resulted in a sense of separation or exclusion from the family story and one to which she often referred. In consequence, she is particularly concerned about her remaining grandparents and wishes to stay in close touch with them. It has also influenced her attitude towards death, especially in relation to anyone in her family carrying donor cards. She believes that making one's body available for medical use after death will result in a similar lack of memorial to that of her grandfather's: in other words, an incomplete story.

Relating this back to the Kitzinger illustration and considering this example in our role as teachers, we must be aware that P brings a particular attitude, based on her experiences, to her understanding of death and the rites entailed. There is a dislocation in her story and her own identity is rendered incomplete. In teaching P, in areas where this subject may arise, it would be inappropriate either to avoid it or to impose particular value judgements upon how death should be treated. This leaves the teacher in something of a dilemma, since facilitating true learning must involve hearing the viewpoints of children and allowing them to evidence their opinion. This is impossible without recourse to a sharing of the experiences and reflections of the children themselves. It is obvious, simply through relating this one example, what a sensitive business the education of the whole child is, and why many of us would wish to shy away from understanding our educational responsibilities in this way. Of course children soon become aware of what sort of discourse the teacher wishes to take place in the classroom and will not reveal such experiences and opinions if the ethos created is not suitable.

However, if we regard children as the ones who possess the fundamental resources for learning within them, then we release a huge potential when we allow these to emerge. Theodore Roszak (1981) refers to this when he states:

> We all bring into school a wholly unexplored, radically unpredictable identity. To educate is to unfold that identity – to unfold it with the utmost delicacy, recognising that it is the most precious resource of our species, the true wealth of the human nation.

One way of approaching this sense of identity is to take account of what we might call the journeying of children through their life experiences. The Greek poet Cavafy has expressed this idea eloquently in his poem 'Ithaca', which recounts the mythical journey of Ulysses as a model for our own progress through life. The first verse is as follows:

13

> When you start on your journey to Ithaca,
> then pray that the road is long,
> full of adventure, full of knowledge.
> Do not fear the Lestrygonians
> and the Cyclops and the angry Poseidon.
> You will never meet such as these on your path,
> if your thoughts remain lofty, if a fine
> emotion touches your body and your spirit.
> You will never meet the Lestrygonians,
> the Cyclops and the fierce Poseidon
> if you do not carry them within your soul,
> if your soul does not raise them up before you.

He concludes:

> And if you find her poor, Ithaca has not defrauded you,
> With the great wisdom you have gained, with so much experience,
> you must surely have understood by then what Ithacas mean.
>
> (Dalven, 1961)

The value of Cavafy's ideas lie in the openness they offer to teachers in the manner in which they introduce children to learning. They suggest that we can initiate children into a love of learning that relates to their own worlds without forcing an adult story upon them. He also rightly suggests that we can all create our own story with its own goals and then evaluate its meaning. If we regard this as a primary aim of education and schooling then we have to be concerned with what children bring to us rather than what we bring to them.

To conclude, the education of the whole child is therefore determined by certain principles which guide our teaching and facilitate children's learning. These are as follows:

- Process, not content, is the key to their development.
- Their storying is the basis of their learning.
- Attitudes determine the ability to learn from others.
- Teachers are facilitators and guides, not necessarily the owners of knowledge.
- Relationships within the classroom are the most significant factor in developing or retarding children's progress.

In Chapter 2 we examine how this is illustrated in practice and introduce the work of the Children and Worldviews Project which seeks to discover how we can best access children's understanding of their experiences and incorporate them into classroom practice.

References

Ashton-Warner, S. (1980) *Teacher.* London, Virago.

Dalven, R. (trans.) (1961) *The Complete Poems of Cavafy.* London, Chatto & Windus.

Fowler, J.W., Nipkow, K. and Schweitzer, F. (eds) (1992) *Stages of Faith and Religious Development: Implications for Church, Education and Society.* London, SCM Press.

Kitzinger, S. (1987) *The Experience of Childbirth.* Harmondsworth, Penguin.

Meek, M., Warlow, A. and Barton, G. (eds) (1977) *The Cool Web: The Pattern of Children's Reading.* London, The Bodley Head.

Roszak, T. (1981) *Person/Planet.* London, Granada.

Wells, G. (1986) *The Meaning Makers: Children Learning Language and Using Language to Learn.* Portsmouth, Hodder and Stoughton.

2 The educational climate and the Children and Worldviews Project

Danny Sullivan and Clive Erricker

Setting a context

Part 1 of the 1988 Education Reform Act attests to the importance of the spiritual, moral, social and cultural developments of all pupils. It is significant that this takes precedence over Part 2 of the Act which focuses on the development of the National Curriculum. However, the reality of life immediately after the Act was that full attention was given by most parties in education to Part 2 of the Act – the National Curriculum. Yet the fact that Part 1 of the Act addressed the spiritual, moral, social and cultural needs of all pupils indicated the rising debate about religious and moral education and a confused sense of children's spirituality. The debate was not helped by different parties within reverting to clichés and stereotypes and often appearing to gain satisfaction from scoring points off one another. In this environment the defence of ideas and positions often took precedence over the rights and needs of children.

Content versus experience?

In dividing the 1988 Act into two parts it could be argued that there was an attempt to separate out knowledge (curriculum) from the pupil's development as a whole person. Following the passing of the Act there was considerable argument concerning the space, time, resources and guidance needed to implement the National Curriculum. Attention was focused on fitting the curriculum into the school timetable. Thus those aspects of the curriculum which could contribute to the development of children as whole persons were marginalized. If mathematics, language and science were the core curriculum and children were to be tested in these subjects, teachers would find it difficult to apportion reasonable time to religious education, art, music and drama. Yet these aspects had the potential to contribute fully to children's religious, spiritual, social and moral development. The danger of producing a dualistic approach to the 1988 Act was evidenced by research at the University of Warwick which indicated that Key Stage 1 teachers were devoting most of their curriculum time to mathematics, language and science. A significant reason given for this was the introduction of testing in all these areas.

Purpose and process

The 1988 Education Reform Act did not set out an explicit philosophy of education, though given the narrow focus on mathematics, language and science, one could detect the heart of a philosophy. Indeed, following the first draft of the National Curriculum (mathematics, language and science), Bishop David Konstant, Chair of the Education Commission within the Roman Catholic community, asked the question 'Mathematics, language and science makes for an educated person – says who?' By 1988 we had moved a long way from secretaries of state like the Conservative Sir Edward Boyle or Labour's Tony Crosland, who found the time and had the inclination to engage in debate about the philosophy of education both with those inside the educational world as well as those outside it.

The idea of the education of the child as a whole person is not a new one but in recent times to address this idea and explore it has been to invite attack and derision. Yet if a child has the right and a need to develop in a religious sense, and also in relation to the spiritual, moral, social and cultural senses, then time will need to be given to enabling this to happen. In order to find that time, something will have to give in what already appears to be an overcrowded timetable. Contained in such a view of children's development is the hope that each child will be enabled and empowered to achieve his or her full potential. Thus, if any key aspect of a child's development is undernourished – for example, the social or the moral – progress towards full potential may well be stunted. Many teachers recognize this reality in the daily life of the classroom when children who may be perfectly capable in academic terms make limited all-round progress because of their undernourishment socially, emotionally, morally and spiritually. Some schools and teachers confront this challenge from the first day the child enters the classroom.

The legacy of child development

In chapter 2 of the Plowden Report, published in 1967, it is stated:

> At the heart of the educational process lies the child. No advances in policy, no acquisitions of new equipment have their desired effect unless they are in harmony with the nature of the child ...
>
> In the last 50 years much work has been done on the physical, emotional and intellectual growth of children. There is a vast array of facts and a number of general principles have been established.
>
> (DES, 1967, vol. 1, para. 9ff.)

The Plowden Report was over 500 pages long. It was a comprehensive survey of the state of education and attempted to address wide-ranging needs. It looked at buildings as well as pupils, and it had a view of teacher training as it did of health and social services.

It is instructive and ironic that those who would place a curriculum rather than the child at the heart of the educational process would not only refer to that opening sentence in chapter 2 of Plowden as if it were fixed in stone but would also choose to ignore the wide-ranging concerns of the whole report. Yet the Conservative Minister for Education, Sir Edward Boyle, commissioned the report in 1963 and it was received by the Labour Minister for Education, Tony

Crosland, in 1966. In his foreword to the report Crosland stated:

> Primary education is the base on which all other education has to be built. Its importance cannot be overestimated.... There can be no doubt that the work done ... with so much diligence and public spirit, will enable decisions to be reached on a more informed basis by those charged with securing the best development of English education within the resources available.

Plowden, while unapologetic about the need for an understanding of child development, paid due attention to the place of the curriculum, and indeed, chapter 17 is devoted to all the subjects of the curriculum. However, the passing of time and the sharp politicization of education have spawned myths about the Plowden Report. There are those who would claim that it said children should learn when and what they want – a statement hard to credit on a reading of its 500 pages. Yet those who would put a 'thing', curriculum, before a person, the child, have succeeded in marginalizing those who would still value a discussion and debate about the philosophy of education, about theories of learning and child development. Stereotyping the work of teacher trainers has been part of this process, while the reality has been that such trainers try to enable student teachers to relate to the contemporary demands and expectations of education.

The Plowden Report simply accorded due place and respect for the integrity of each child. It recognized the deep potential within each child and it celebrated the ability of children to bring a great deal of their own experience to the learning process as well as to take much from it.

Where to now?

Perhaps we should be appropriately grateful that the 1988 Act reasserted the place of the spiritual, moral, social and cultural development of all pupils. For, since Plowden, education has gone through a period when sound and balanced ideas have been ignored or jettisoned if they appeared inimical to the god of management of the curriculum. There has not been the luxury of debate as to how we educate and why. Part 1 of the Act allows that debate to re-emerge, albeit there are those who would still like to deliver very prescriptive solutions.

Recent information from the Teacher Training Agency suggests that if nothing is done, schools will be 30,000 teachers short by the year 2000. Part of the shortage is due to the serious haemorrhage of able teachers through sickness and early retirement. Much of this can be related to a general feeling within the profession of disaffection and poor morale. This is understandable when for some years there has been constant instability and teachers appear to have been fair game for politicians on all sides. The politicization of education has made it very difficult for a rational and reasonable exchange of views to take place. Both headteachers and teachers regret the lack of time available just to be with children, to listen to them as individuals, to recognize and acknowledge with some humility what their pupils may already have to bring to the world of the school and the classroom. There is a danger that the National Curriculum is reducing listening to children to an attainment target and, in light of that, it has potentially serious effects on children's development.

Margaret Donaldson, through her books *Children's Minds* and *Human Minds* (Donaldson, 1978, 1993), has argued for a middle path between a child-centred approach and a curriculum-centred approach to learning. Bennett and Galton in their diverse ways wish to raise the profile of teaching methodology, while others like Armstrong and Rowland have focused on observing children on the setting of the classroom through longitudinal studies. Violet Madge in her study *Children in Search of Meaning* (1965) allowed children to speak for themselves. All these studies have contributed to a deeper understanding of the learning process, but perhaps Violet Madge's was most successful in allowing the children's authentic voices to be heard.

The Children and Worldviews Research Project set out to listen to children as openly and sensitively as it could.

The Children and Worldviews Research Project

From the outset the project wished to work with pupils and teachers in a variety of schools. The team members recognized and valued the high commitment of teachers and hoped through the project to produce practical ideas and resources for working with pupils in areas of their growth and development which were both profoundly deep and sensitive. Team members have worked with rural schools and inner city schools, church schools and state schools, schools with a wide multicultural and multifaith mix, and schools which lack such a perspective.

The project set out to listen to children in settings where they feel at ease – whether this be the classroom, a playground or, in one instance, a rubbish dump! The Children and Worldviews Research project has approached listening to children through the use of story, poetry and the discussion of themes which has, wherever possible, allowed the children to set the agenda. At each stage the team has discussed with schools and teachers what children have been saying and it is this evidence which has created a real sense of emerging understanding.

From these interviews and discussions it is hoped that appropriate classroom material can be produced which will be useful to both teachers and pupils. Throughout the project the children consistently inform, stimulate, challenge and provoke our thinking. The project appeals for greater openness and open-endedness in relating to children. It would suggest that if one uses an instruction manual approach to teaching and learning, then one should not be surprised by the limited outcome. The project values and affirms the ability of children to be imaginative, poetic and to live, in a natural way, life's rich narrative as they find it in the worlds in which they move. Through engaging with and listening to the children, the team

21

has had the privilege of being invited to experience the rich tapestry of their lives. It often appeared that they chose to protect this rich tapestry, and the experiences within it, from the world of adults. They seem to be able to have unique experiences, and to create their own stories and histories away from the adult world.

The project recognizes that much of this rich tapestry could make an enormous contribution within the field of spiritual, moral, social and cultural development. Thus two challenges confront it:

- To persuade children that it is valuable and worthwhile to bring their narratives, histories and experiences into the adult world, thus at times teaching the adults.
- To persuade teachers that a context and environment can be created within the classroom to enable this to happen, thus freeing the teacher and the children.

To fail to address these challenges would simply validate the heartfelt accusation of one of the 11-year-olds in the project: 'Adults just don't listen to children.'

The project emerged, fittingly, from conversation initiated by the youngest child of two of the authors. It was P, mentioned in Chapter 1 of this book, who alerted us to the fact that children develop their own awareness of events and seek to understand them in the context of their experience at an early age. We only become aware of this when they seek to communicate it. However, as so often happens, we, the teachers and parents, are too busy or preoccupied to spare the time to respond and encourage their thinking. As a consequence, their thoughts lie buried and the effect can be that we do not discover until later in life what potential has lain dormant or, in certain cases, what damage may arise as a result of neglect. Conversations with P convinced us of the importance of carrying out further research in a more formal way. As a consequence, the Children and Worldviews Project was conceived and, by the spring of 1993, actually born, when interviewing began in our first school. In September 1993 it was funded by three higher education institutions:

Chichester Institute, LSU College, Southampton, and King Alfred's College, Winchester. In May 1994 it appointed its first research assistant. At the time of writing (February 1996) it has appointed a further research student. These appointments will result in the production of two PhDs which will contribute subsequent research information to that included in this work. A short-term bursary given to Mandy Fletcher has resulted in her contribution on the children of New Age parents (Chapter 9).

The basis on which the research has been conducted is described in Chapter 3, but the overall results of the project so far can be given some attention here. This will help the reader to understand what is to follow in the chapters included in Section Two of this book and why we have decided to present our research in this way. Most research is conducted in the context of a defined body of knowledge which, educationally, will relate to a specific curriculum area. This research was unable to fit into that context. It is research into children's thinking, but not to identify stages which their thinking has reached measured according to predetermined criteria relating to rationality, intelligence or moral maturity. We rejected such schematized approaches on the basis that we were not concerned with children's ability to think according to prescribed expectations. We were concerned to know how well they were able to construct explanations of events and strategies for dealing with issues that arose in their personal lives. We also wished to establish how far schools did or could play a part in facilitating their thinking and development in this respect.

The present situation

We were, and still are, aware that educational priorities do not lie in this direction but that new impetus has been given through the work of the School Curriculum Assessment Authority and its conference on Education for Adult Life, which targeted spiritual and moral development (January

23

1996), and the decision to inspect schools in this area of provision through OFSTED. What concerns us is how we arrive at the criteria for inspection and how we come to know what it is that schools are meant to be developing. The object of our research is at least to inform the way in which these questions are addressed. While applauding the initiatives taken so far, it is important to ensure a critical scrutiny of such developments in order that the outcome may truly benefit children's learning. If we examine the speech of SCAA's Chief Executive at the conference and the discussion paper itself, they provide clues as to the direction of present thinking.

We wish to highlight certain statements made by Nick Tate that offer grounds for concern. The thrust of the argument he presents in his speech concerns the erosion of moral values through the acceptance of a pervasive relativism. This he finds located in the views of young people who believe that moral opinion cannot be related to any notion of absolute values. At the same time he quotes an example of quantitative research which evidences that

> young people are more likely to find life worth living, to think it has a purpose, and to show concern for others and for the environment if they are either practising or non practising believers.

(The research carried out referred specifically to Christian believers.) He identifies relativism as a dragon that needs to be slain. He identifies personal and social education as a part cause of this decline into moral relativism through its emphasis on the promotion of pupils' self-esteem. He identifies religious education as a vehicle for the reinstatement of moral values and spiritual education through delivering the entitlement of young people to learn about Christianity, as well as about the other main religions. This, he suggests, will provide them with important ways of understanding themselves and the world in which they live. He identifies children's spiritual development as being as important as 'the origin of the will to do what is right'. He cites the Archbishop of Canterbury's statement that 'as people move further away from [the legacy of a deep, residual belief in God] they find it more and more difficult to give a substantial basis for why they should be good'. He views pejoratively the notion that Blur or *Neighbours* should be valued by young people on a par with Shakespeare or Schubert. He cites postmodern ideas as a specific reason for cultural fragmentation and the success of specific urban schools as being based on an 'explicit and sustained commitment to core values'. His explicit aim is a return to promoting the development of a virtuous society based on the transmission of a set of rules, precepts and principles.

The grounds for our concern rest on both the tone of the speech and the assumptions of its argument. At the conference in a seminar group following the speech, delegates were angry at the suggestion that schools and teachers were somehow responsible for this decline and that the importance of encouraging pupils' self-esteem should be denigrated. The emphasis of the speech was on the importance of telling young people how they should behave and what values they should have. This was related to the importance of promoting a belief in God, in which an emphasis on the Christian God was implicitly placed. There was also an emphasis on the notion of spiritual development being valuable only in the service of moral education, which was defined as fostering already prescribed moral principles or values, which schools and society had clearly failed to do in recent educational history. Despite the call for a forum to discuss the issues surrounding these subjects and practical action, the agenda was fixed and the voices of teachers, let alone children, played a marginal part.

When we refer to the discussion paper itself in the light of Nick Tate's speech, further concerns arise. The discussion paper clearly distinguishes between spiritual and moral development and one feature of the distinction is the openness of the descriptions of aspects of spiritual development in contrast to those more prescriptive elements listed under moral development. The aspects of spiritual development refer to the development of personal beliefs, being inspired by the natural world, the belief that one's inner resources provide the ability to rise above everyday experiences, responding to challenging experiences such as beauty, suffering and death, the ability to build up relationships and other factors which our conversations with children reveal as being of utmost importance to them. They find exploring such themes challenging and significant because by doing so they raise issues in their own experience which they are striving to resolve.

The elements of moral development cited are:

- the will to behave morally as a point of principle;
- knowledge of the codes and conventions of conduct agreed by society;
- knowledge and understanding of the criteria put forward as a basis for making responsible judgements on moral issues;
- the ability to make judgements on moral issues.

These issues are supported by the statements that 'children need to know the difference between right and wrong', 'schools should be expected to uphold moral absolutes' and 'young children rarely have the ability or experience to make their own decisions as to what is right and wrong'. While this selective quoting can lead to misinterpretation, it does appear that there is a discrepancy between what we are asking of children under spiritual development and what we require of them with regard to moral development, the difficulty lying in the assumption that the exploration of the former will lead to acceptance of the prescriptions entailed in the latter. This ignores the complexity of moral decision-making and the capacity of children to engage in arriving at moral conclusions as a result of thinking through issues germane to their own experience. Further, it does not recognize that the reasons why children sometimes do not behave morally, as is the case with adults, are due not to a lack of the capacity to reason or an ignorance of moral codes, but because the nature of their experience has resulted in a sense of resentment towards those in authority who prescribe forms of behaviour that seem to

The following sections explain how we tried to overcome these problems.

1. The lack of a clear hypothesis

Scientific research usually begins with an idea of the nature of the problem. This is then refined to produce a research question and the next stage is to speculate on what the answer to that research question might be. The investigation that follows is an attempt to prove or disprove that answer. The answer proposed is called a hypothesis. In the kind of research that is carried out by this project the above procedure is not really feasible. A hypothesis cannot be formulated in clear terms because of the complexity of the situations and the impossibility of the control of variables. The researcher needs to enter the field with a holistic approach and to be both aware of, and to appreciate the value of, all the sources of data, and to find the nature of the question within those data. Other researchers have found that they must begin with a sense of direction, that is, an idea of the questions to which answers may be required, but those questions are allowed to grow and change as the research advances. In *Doing Qualitative Research: Circles Within Circles,* Margot Ely says,

> For most of us, the questions shift, specify and change from the very beginning in a cyclical process as the [research] grows, is thought about, analysed, and provides further direction for the study. This is certainly different from positivistic research in which questions are posed at the start and do not change, and, in this difference, it is often discomfiting. It takes a certain emotional sturdiness for any researcher, but particularly a beginning one, not to reach too quickly and too firmly for 'the' question. It takes conviction and confidence to collect and examine one's data with the view that the questions can and should change, and to love that possibility. (Ely *et al.*, 1991, p. 31)

This approach, that is, of finding the questions in the data as you go along, has been put forward as 'Grounded Theory' by Glaser and Strauss in their book *The Discovery of Grounded Theory* (1967). According to this theory, it is important that the researcher should be allowed to revise and adapt the research question as the data collection progresses, instead of adhering tightly to the original hypothesis. The most obvious problem with the latter approach is that the researcher can be blinded to anything which falls outside of the original remit, ignoring as unimportant or perhaps inaccurate any data which do not conform. This means that researchers can remain startlingly conformist, and can spend their time confirming and refining the so-called 'great-man theories' instead of being innovative.

Thus, in the work of the project, we tried to enter the field of research, that is, we went to talk to children, with no definite ideas of what we were looking for or what we would find. We had identified our area of interest. We wanted to know what children felt was important in their lives; in other words, what coloured the way they looked at the world and thus what affected the way they learned. We believed we had to listen to the children and identify the important things to follow up in what they said. We then expected to, and did, find a narrower focus as the data were collected and categories found which guided the interpretation of the data.

2. The complexity of the research situation

We have already explained the complex nature of educational research, or indeed any research which involves human beings. (Children tend to be even more difficult to find out about because they are not even necessarily co-operative.) Part of the problem lies in the identification and control of all the possible variables and the other part is in the question of the quantification of the results of the research. It is possible to ask many different people the same questions and get a general sense of the opinions and knowledge of that group of people. The data that you collect can be expressed as statistics and graphs and they are easy to see and appreciate. However, for the sake of that simplicity and accessibility, this approach ignores the complexity which we have identified. We felt that we would not be able to gather data which were meaningful or relevant by this means, that is, by using questionnaires. We also felt that it was not practically feasible to use this method with young children aged between 5 and 11 who would not be able to complete a questionnaire without adult assistance, which would then obviously alter any responses. The method of using questionnaires, statistics and graphs is the sociological and educational version of quantitative research; that is, research which produces numbers as its results. We decided to use a methodology which has been described in a number of ways – qualitative, ethnographic and naturalistic are just three examples. Although no single precise definition has been formulated, a number of common characteristics can be identified in the research which uses this methodology, and which therefore link the terms together. These common characteristics have been listed by Bogden and Biklen in their book *Qualitative Research for Education* (1982), though they note that not all studies exhibit all of these traits.

They say that qualitative research

- has the natural setting as the direct source of data and the researcher as the key instrument. To divorce the act, word or gesture from its context is to lose sight of its significance;
- is descriptive – words and pictures rather than numbers;
- is concerned with process rather than simply the outcomes or problems;
- is inductively analysed – abstractions are built as the particulars are grouped together;
- has meaning as an essential concern.

The flexibility and openness of this qualitative research framework suited our investigation extremely well and answered many of our concerns. In addition, we felt that our methodology needed to be child-centred – allowing the children space and time in which to express themselves freely and without the hindrances of us as adults presuming to give them the appropriate tools and language. We decided that this approach would allow us to share in and understand the thoughts and concepts of the children. However, we did accept that this child-centred approach needed to be balanced by an aspect of research which relies on the observer's rather than the actor's perspective. This is so that the researcher can make connections which the children would find either inappropriate or meaningless, between stories and experiences described by them.

3. The impossibility of an objective stance by the researcher

As we said earlier, we understood that a completely objective stance by a researcher is impossible, and that if the research was to be what we understood as honest, we would have to take the subjectivity of the researcher into account. However, understanding that point philosophically, and putting that principle into action practically, are two completely different tasks.

We consulted a book referred to briefly earlier (Ely *et al.*, 1991). They suggested that this problem should be met head on, and that the approach to research could 'enable the researcher to be creative, exploring new ideas that could take shape via intuition, vision and personal experience, *and* to be analytical, so as to imbue that experience with meaning' (p. 107). The affective component could be acknowledged without demeaning the results of the research. This seemed to be the approach which we were looking for, but we had to establish how to put it into action. The key aspect of the acknowledgement of our own subjectivity was to examine how we felt about actually doing the research, and to record our feelings in a research log. As Jackie Storm says:

> Learn to live with your fears and insecurities. They are part of the process. Make a note of your paranoia. Write it down in your log; use it as a source of information. You are here to observe what is going on, and your personal thoughts and feelings are one part of the total picture. To deny our feelings would be to shut out one large chunk of reality. (Ely *et al.*, 1991, p. 111)

Thus we all kept research logs, which meant that when we went into a school to talk to children or to teachers, we wrote how we felt about anticipating the task, how we felt while carrying it out, and our feelings afterwards. Any other thoughts we had at any time about the research were also recorded. As well as helping us to acknowledge our own anxieties, this process also helped us to remember everything that happened when we were with the children or teachers which may have affected what they said. The thoughts that we had in between actually collecting the data helped us when we came to the analysis of the interviews.

These logs were highly personal documents, and the members of the team chose whether they wished to share them with others. Discussing the research in detail, and perhaps sharing the logs, was another way of allowing our subjectivity to be taken into account.

As you can tell from Jackie Storm's quote above, doing this kind of research carries a risk. There is a sense in which the acknowledgement of subjectivity exposes the researcher as a fallible human being, with all the doubts and fears that you might expect, though these doubts and fears can be very successfully hidden behind the mask of objectivity, where the work that the researcher does is separate from the researcher as a person. But we felt that the essence of our research was to ask children to open themselves to us, to tell us highly personal and quite often secret things, and it was only fair that we should be as open, if not to the children, at least in what we wrote about them. Philosophically, we felt that it was the right way to approach the work.

Our practical methodology

We decided to gain access to children through the schools they attended. All members of the research team were connected to the educational world and therefore knew schools and teachers personally. We needed to make contact with schools and ask if the headteacher minded us coming into the school and interviewing the children. We asked headteachers whose approach to their work was child-centred and whose philosophy we felt would be in tune with ours. We also tried to use a variety of schools in different areas, and some schools with religious affiliation and some without. We talked to the head-teachers and explained the nature of the research and the way in which we wanted to collect our data. We offered to talk to or to send letters to governors and parents if necessary, to explain what we were doing. We offered open access to the data.

The selection of the children whom we interviewed we discussed with the headteacher. We needed children who were willing to talk to us and who would respond to the social situation of a group interview. We prefered to interview the children in small groups because we felt that this was less intimidating than a one-to-one arrangement. In pilot studies four or five children appeared to be the best number, allowing all the children a chance to talk, but encouraging discussion between the children as well as with the researcher.

We talked to the children at the school and where it was possible to be private. This has led to some complications, where children have been distracted by books and other resources available in the room chosen. On the one occasion when children were interviewed in the school staffroom, it took a long time for them to overcome the fascination of being in a usually forbidden place. The interviews were not structured, but we used certain questions or stimuli to start the children thinking in the required area. Sometimes we used books or pictures, or asked them to draw something. One researcher even took the children for a walk around the school or the neighbourhood and talked to them as they walked. All the conversations were recorded and transcribed later. We all tried to pick up on interesting comments that the children made.

We also tried to talk to the teachers about the children, though this was not always formally done. This was a means of triangulating the data, making a richer and more complete picture of each child.

In general, we felt very privileged to be able to spend time with young children, and to be allowed to encourage them to talk about their feelings, beliefs and values. They demonstrated to us that they are capable of great depth of thought and that they can carry out sophisticated arguments among themselves as long as they are given credit for being able to do this, and their ideas are afforded the respect they deserve.

Ethics

We felt that this subject required a section of its own, because the issue of ethics pervades the whole of the research process. As Margot Ely says, the whole of qualitative research is an 'ethical endeavour':

> striving to be faithful to another's viewpoint is striving to be ethical. Striving to maintain confidentiality is striving to be ethical. Striving to be trustworthy is striving to be ethical. It is impossible to confine ethical considerations ... actually they are present from the beginning and are woven throughout every step of the methodology.   (Ely *et al.*, 1991, p. 218)

While we were carrying out the research we identified two broad areas of ethical concern:

1. For the integrity of the research itself;
2. For the participants.

In order to maintain the integrity of the research we recognized the need to be aware of the quality, value and honesty of our research and our trustworthiness as researchers. This meant that we had to carry out the research as fairly and accurately as possible, checking each other's assumptions and conclusions, how we involved both adults and children in the research process, and how we communicated the results.

As far as the participants were concerned we felt we had to preserve the anonymity of the children and schools concerned as a matter of necessity. We also acknowledged that consent for the research reached beyond the teachers and headteachers and parents involved, and also included the informed consent of the children themselves, respecting their wishes if they did not wish to be taped or to contribute to group discussions. It has to be recognized that this kind of research can occasionally reveal something of real concern in a child's life, and decisions as to what to do about this information, given freely by a child in a situation of trust, are very difficult to make.

Conclusion

The methodology used by members of the project team had at its heart the philosophy described above, and the way in which we carried it out conformed more or less to the above format. However, each of us entered a unique situation, and responded to that situation in our own subjective ways, as you will see when you read Section Two of this book. However, the overriding principle that we bore in mind is that offered by Dick DeLuca:

> The best advice anyone can give is LISTEN, LISTEN – and LISTEN MORE. (Ely *et al.*, 1991, p. 66)

References

Bogden, R. and Biklen, S. (1982) *Qualitative Research for Education.* Boston, Allyn & Bacon.

Ely, M., Anzul, M., Friedman, T., Garner, D. and McCormack, A. (1991) *Doing Qualitative Research: Circles Within Circles.* London, Falmer Press.

Glaser, B.D. and Strauss, A.K. (1967) *The Discovery of Grounded Theory.* Chicago, Aldine.

Section Two

The research process

4 Children's experience of conflict and loss

Clive Erricker

The situation

I visited this school initially at the request of the headteacher after she had attended an in-service course on Buddhism and meditation in the primary school. Her concern was to teach children to relax and calm down in order to help them learn. My job was to help them to do this through story and reflection. As a result of this we realized how important it was to investigate the children's own thinking and the experiences that influenced their ability to learn. Often the children came to school in a stressed condition because of the circumstances of their home lives, and this resulted in difficulties within the classroom and their relationships with each other. Investigating what they brought to school seemed to be a way in which we could make it easier for them to learn and resolve some of the difficulties they were experiencing. Consequently, our research began at this school in 1993 and with these children, focusing on conflict and loss.

The children were 7 years of age and were interviewed in groups of between four and six, and subsequently in pairs. They were selected from one class which, like others in this inner city school, contained a high proportion of children with emotional and learning difficulties. All the children were eager to be interviewed and this presented some problems, partly because of a lack of communication skills – some children could not conduct proper conversations – and partly because a number of the children presented difficulties in their demands for attention. Nearly all the children in the class were interviewed once in the larger groups. Others were selected for further interviews in pairs on the basis of their contributions and, through discussion with the class teachers (there were two, both part-time) and the headteacher, on the basis of the value the process would have for the children as individuals. The pairings were largely decided according to the relationships between the children involved – we wanted children to speak freely in the presence of a friend and to talk about opinions and experiences that they could easily share, though not necessarily agree upon.

This chapter largely examines the results of the paired interviews with six children: three girls – V, N and K – and three boys – B, C and M. In part it has a longitudinal aspect, since we interviewed again one-and-a-half years later, in spring 1995, when the children were aged 9, or 10 (in the case of M). These interviews were again conducted in pairs; however, this excluded C because by this time he had left the school as a result of difficulties with his behaviour. It is worth noting that the headteacher also left during this period. She retired on the grounds of ill-heath, but was still involved with the research through advising and commenting on the recorded conversations and giving us information that contextualized them in the larger world of school, family and community. The new headteacher, G, previously the deputy headteacher, provided the same encouragement and an equal amount of time and support in working towards interpretations and conclusions. The early retirement of the first headteacher is an indication that there are some schools, such as this one, where as a teacher you put your health on the line in your commitment to the children's education, as well as bringing a particular professional expertise to your job. It was essential to the overall worth of our work that the staff involved recognized that we also contributed to the development of the children in their care.

The interviews

In our initial interviews the choice of a relevant stimulus was crucial. We asked the children to respond to an engaging but brief focus for their reflection. In other schools this was varied to include initial questions but, in this case, we considered that the children needed a narrative to respond to. In each of the group interviews we used the following poem by Brian Patten:

Looking for Dad

Whenever Mum and Dad
were full of gloom
they always yelled,
'TIDY UP YOUR ROOM!'
Just because my comics were
scattered here and
everywhere and
because I did not care
where I left my underwear
they yelled, 'WE'LL SEND YOU TO
A HOUSE OF CORRECTION
IF YOU DON'T TIDY UP
YOUR STAMP COLLECTION!'
Then one day they
could not care less
about the room's
awful mess.
They seemed more intent
on a domestic argument.
They both looked glum
and instead of me Dad
screeched at Mum.
One night when I
went to bed he
simply vanished.
(ten past seven, tenth of June.)
I had not tidied
up my room because
I too was
full of gloom.

That night I dreamt
Dad was hidden
beneath the things
I'd been given.
In my dream
I was in despair
and flung about
my underwear
but could not find
him anywhere.
I looked for him
lots and lots
beneath crumpled sheets
and old robots.
I looked in cupboards
and in shoes.
I looked up all
the chimney flues.
I remembered how
he'd seemed to be
unhappier than
even me. When I woke I knew
it was not my room
that filled Mum and Dad
with so much gloom.
Now I stare at all
my old toy cars
and carpets stained
with old Mars bars
and hope he will
come back soon
and admire my very tidy room.
(It is now the twenty-ninth of June.)

The children reacted to this poem in various ways. I wish to
chart the responses, in particular those of V and B, and to indicate the way in which their comments, made in the context of
the first group, were elaborated upon in the later interviews
which traced the way in which loss was woven into the pattern
of their lives. In presenting these responses we have sometimes

taken the original interview transcripts and removed the interviewer's interventions. This has enabled us to present the children's own narratives without interruption.

V's response

V's response was prefaced by another child, J, explaining that she thought Dad had gone to heaven. V then picked up this idea and elaborated on it in relation to the death of her grandmother.

Q: Where do you think Dad has gone?

J: Up in heaven.

Q: J, tell me what happens when you go up to heaven.

J: You see God and that.

V: I think that in heaven you can ride a white pony and have marshmallows. Before my nan died she told me lots of things because she knew she was going to die and she told me about all the things she was going to do and she said she was going to send me a postcard. Before she went she gave me a piece of paper and stuck a photograph on it. I've still got it.

She said she would be happy and she wanted me to be happy when she died. On that day she got a picture of her and all the family, stuck it on a postcard and wrote on the back 'I'll see you in your heart'. Now she's always with me. Now I talk to her all the time. I talk to her when I'm lonely. When I've argued with my friends I go and sit on the wall and think about her and talk to her. When I get fed up I sit there and talk to her about my friends. She tells me that she's riding on things. She says she's having a really nice time. She says she's going to ring me up. She says things in my head, she rings up my brain and talks to me. When she went up in heaven she took one of her special secrets. She took it with her and she can just ring me up, it's clever. This special secret makes her able to do that.

I keep on wanting to tell people things but they don't

understand. I know everyone's in heaven who has died. Grandma tells me. She works in a cleaners. She washes all the clouds in heaven. She's got lots and lots of friends in heaven. She hopes we'll stay alive a long time but she wants me to go up there to see her. I'd like to go and see her but if you go up there you've got to stay there. You can't go unless you've died. Heaven is high, high in the sky, it's higher than space.

I've never worried about these things. I just keep it in my heart. It's not a problem. It makes me quite sad they [people] don't believe. But when God talks to them they will know. We are very, very lucky that just some people care in this world. Like me and my friends and everybody in this school, I hope, we care, we keeps this planet going. I think heaven is part of this planet.

My nan was burnt when she died, cremated. I think that's better than worms coming into your coffin.

V's response is interesting for a number of reasons; these are as follows:

- Because she was prepared to make such a personal statement in the presence of other children, not just her own friends.
- Because she makes it with conviction. She is committed to an interpretation of her grandmother's death that is more than a fanciful idea.
- Because of the metaphorical language she uses which is necessary to an interpretation and communication of her experience.
- Because through this explanation she clearly gains empowerment.
- Because the explanation necessitates further reflection on metaphysical ideas related to her grandmother's continued existence. Thus God, the world and the sustaining power of love become important.
- Because childlike and rather Disneyesque imagery becomes used for and functions to provide a vehicle for a more profound personal purpose: to locate the possibility of her continued relationship with her grandmother beyond death.
- Because it points to the significance of a particular traumatic experience in generating and utilizing a child's reflective capabilities in a way that would not have focused them otherwise.

- Because her explanation does not depend on a use of any overtly religious or Christian doctrine to substantiate her views, suggesting that a nurturing in explicitly Christian ideas has not been necessary to the creation of her own explanation.

Subsequently, we came to recognize the influence of her other grandmother in providing some of the imagery she used, but, even more importantly, it was the relationships established within her immediate family, the grandparents and her mother, which facilitated what we may call her meaning making. This also allowed her to come to terms with a subsequent death, that of her grandfather, as she explains:

V: My grandmother used to go along to where you get poppies. Got a thousand poppies at home as a memory of grandad. I've got my grandad's bed. We've got his special belongings and we're going to sell the rest of his stuff at a car boot sale with my toys when I was young. We're going to sell the possessions that weren't special to him.

We've got a horse. He had a horse when he was a boy. His own real horse. He had a statue of it made, to remember his horse. I've got his horse now. I take it everywhere but not to school. Then I know my grandad's with me.

Q: Is he really with you?

V: (*nods*) I feel I'm touching him now. When I want to see him one more time I gaze at the horse and imagine I can see him. Other times it's just a horse to me. And the other day I went to a funeral parlour. I took a carnation and made my own card and I just wanted to see him one more time. I was just begging to go to the funeral. I went to the funeral parlour and I put the carnation in his hand.

Q: How was he?

V: He was dressed in white. He had a very precious gold belt around his waist. It was like monks wear. He was lying in the coffin.

49

Q: How did that feel?

V: He was asleep. Yes, asleep to me.

Q: Are you glad you did that?

V: Yea, made me feel a lot better. I didn't cry after that. I didn't cry at all while I was there. I knew he was asleep.

V's grandfather died in autumn 1993. When interviewed at that time she had been willing to speak about her grandmother's death (her grandmother had died some years before) but initially not of her grandfather's. She had begun our second interview by saying:

> I'm very upset. Just caught asthma and my grandad's just died.

As the interview progressed she and N, with whom she was paired, spoke about the need to care for animals and the earth and then V unexpectedly returned to her grandad's death and related the above story. However, V did not immediately relate her grandmother's and grandfather's after-life stories as being the same, but on further enquiry she offered this explanation:

V: He was asleep, yes asleep to me.

Q: And now, where is he?

V: He had, not a funeral, a cremation.

Q: Are you glad you did that?

V: Yes, made me feel a lot better. I didn't cry after that. I didn't cry at all while I was there. I knew he was asleep.

Q: Is he still asleep?

V: Yea, but he's just buried, that's all. He'll sleep for a hundred years.

Q: Then what will happen?

V: Nothing, he'll just be there

Q: He hasn't gone to join your grandma?

V: Yea.

Q: Is he in heaven?

V: Yea, but he'll always be asleep. But he'll be doing things. He'll be asleep to me like my grandma is, but um, it'll be the same as my nan, he'll be taking care of the animals.

If we now analyse the picture presented by V so far, it has the following characteristics:

- The world is sustained by caring.
- Heaven is a part of this world but a separate part.
- When God speaks to people they will know this is true.
- Her grandmother can speak to her from heaven.
- Her grandmother and grandfather are both asleep but both doing things.
- She keeps in touch with them through the things that they gave her and by going off and being alone with them.

What seems to matter most, in both cases, is that both grandparents are in touch with her in some way, whether through the horse or the postcard with the photograph on it, and that they are happy or at peace. V did not see her dead grandmother, but she did see her dead grandfather. As a consequence, it seems, her image of him asleep is important in the way that she is able to remember him, whereas her way of remembering her grandmother is to picture her as actively doing those things she remembered her doing during her life. This raises important questions as to how children deal with death. In V's case she creates imaginative scenes which she can relate to the memories she has of her dead grandparents. In her grandfather's case it is significant that she was allowed to see him before he was buried and to go through the ritual of saying goodbye. The memory of events that have occurred before and after death are the basis on which she can relate her continued contact with her grandparents and affirm that they are all right. Without these images, it seems, bereavement would be a wholly negative and disempowering experience for her. Her capacity to relate the event of death depended upon the conversation with her grandmother before she died and being allowed to see her dead grandfather 'asleep'. These facilitating events enabled her to carry the thread of her story across the trauma of the death of a loved one because life before death and whatever happened after death were both familiar to her, and it was possible for her to contextualize them within her experiences of sleep and daily activity. This does not mean that she confuses sleep and death; rather, she uses sleep as a metaphor for death by saying 'he'll be asleep to me like my grandma is'. It is also important to stress that she does not arrive at this idea because she has been told about it; rather, she had to witness it as a means of constructing her own explanation. The other sustaining facet of her story is that, though asleep, they are both still active. This apparent contradiction does not prove difficult for her.

The function of these two images is crucial to recognizing their value. Sleep is peace, activity is life. What V projects on to her grandparents after death is that they are in a peaceful and happy situation. The concept coined for this is being in heaven. Thus the logical contradiction is dispelled, and she can cope with their death. This understanding is provisional, it meets her present needs and is constructed partly as a result of talking through the situation. She does not come to the conversations having fully resolved the issue. What matters is going through the process, not arriving at certain solutions.

Eighteen months after this interview V was interviewed with K, who had also lost her grandfather.

V: I was talking to my grandad during the night.
K: I always talk to mine.
Q: You always talk to your grandad?
K: I always talk to my grandad.
Q: Even though he's dead?
K: Yea.
V: We've talked about that before.
Q: We did didn't we, yea. How do you do that, K?
K: I just find a photo and I just talk to him like that.
Q: Right, what sort of things do you say?
K: I say I wish it weren't you, I wish it was someone else [who died].

At the end of this interview, during which V had been largely silent on the subject of her grandfather, she cried. It seems she had gone through the stage of wishing to talk about it. The grief still remained but was better left unexpressed.

C and M

Subsequent to the initial interviews C and M were paired together. They were different in many ways, M being quite quiet and C a restless and difficult child. Nevertheless they were friends, and it was hoped that they would be willing to talk openly in each other's company.

As an initial stimulus they were asked to draw a circle and put into it a picture of something or someone who mattered to them. M drew two figures holding a bag. C did not want to draw anything, because he felt he was not good at drawing. While M drew, C sat on a cushion but in a very animated fashion. He could not keep still and was soon moving around the room playing with different pieces of equipment.

M explained his picture.

M's story

I like helping old people, carrying their food and help them get up the stairs because they're old and they can't live very long, old people. When they die people feel sad. My grandad died the other day. I think he had a heart attack in the hospital. I think he had cancer in his lungs and he had bad ribs. I was bringing him letters saying get well soon but he didn't get well, he died. He went in a deep sleep and he died. That was about six months ago, I don't remember all of it. My grandad's in the grave now. We often go up to the grave to see him. I'll always be in touch with my grandad. I pray for him every night before I go to bed. I say please God could you make my grandad be alive soon. I want to see him.

I believe in God and that you should be good, but when people die I think life just stop for them. We're all getting older, every year we're growing dead. Grown-ups get older and we get older. That makes me feel sad, I wish I was a baby and then I would live a bit longer, I'd like to stay 8, you've got more toys. When I grow up I want to stay 8. It's not good for old people because they die soon and it's not so good for the other people. We're lucky but we might die or something.

53

M's explanation indicated a very different attitude to death from that of V:

- Ageing was a progression towards death and he wished to remain young.
- Death was a separation, despite the wish to still be in touch with his grandfather.
- Prayer was possible but not a means of changing the situation.

M comes from a practising Roman Catholic family but does not enjoy going to church or Sunday School.

After M had commented on the meaning of his picture C tried to offer him consolation.

C: He's still alive M, he's an angel.

M: I know, he's flying around now probably.

Q: Where are the angels, C, are they with us or somewhere else?

C: At night they come. They're in the air. They never come in your house.

M: They look in through the window.

C: When my mum dies I'll put some blood in her and she'll stay alive a bit longer. Cos I don't want her to die. When my mum dies I might want to go with her.

M: Yea, stab yourself.

C: I'm not too scared to do it you know, I'll do it right now ... yea, I'm not allowed to am I?

Q: Is that because you love your mum?

C: (*nods*)

Q: And what do you think will happen to your mum when she dies?

C: She'll become an angel. I'll want to come and see what she'll be like. I'll wait for her. I'll wait for a long time till I dies and then I'll be the same.

C's attempt to provide M with a more positive explanation is interesting. It draws on his Caribbean Pentecostalist background, though church attendance is not a regular feature of his family life. He draws on supernatural images, most specifically the role of angels, to change M's attitude. He is sensitive to M's bereavement and recognizes that if it happened to him, through his mother dying (he has no father at home), he would find the loss impossible to accept. M goes along with the explanation but is not convinced by it. The conversation changes from real issues to one unrelated to his experience.

C's explanation fits with the way in which he interprets the everyday situations he finds himself in.

C's story

I like having a gang but I can't tell you who's in my gang, it's a secret. We walk about the estate and people get scared of me. They try to take us on but there's more of us and there are big boys. L's a big boy and he can't take us on. D's a trouble-maker on the estate. His dad's name's S and he's in prison. When he's in prison we beat D up. D's big and he tries to get us to do some shoplifting. I beat him up at the disco and he was bleeding. He felt gutted.

I've got a book with stories about God in it, a kiddies' Bible. My mum and dad used to go to church and I believe in God. I think you should and there's a good reason to – he gives you food and all that and he's the one who made us. You should believe in God and God the father as well.

If you believe in God you have to be good. But D, he's on the devil's side, he nicks motorbikes and all that you see. He pushed W into the river and me, P, I and S jumped into the river and saved him. If you talk about a devil the devil swoops down somewhere in your room and tries to get you to do things. He tries to get you to hurt the angel in the other ear. The devil sits on my shoulder and he says things and he flies away and I've killed the devil I have. But he still sometimes whispers in my ear to tell me naughty things.

When people die I think they go back to God and become an angel. It is true, I've got a big Bible. The angels come at night, they're in the air. They never come in your house. When my mum dies I'll put some blood in her and she'll stay alive a bit longer. Cos I don't want her to die. When my mum dies I might want to go with her. I'm not too scared to do it you know, I'll do it because I love her, but I'm not allowed to am I? When she does die she'll become an angel. I'll want to come and see what she'll be like. I'll wait for her. I'll wait for a long time till I dies and then I'll be the same.

For C the world is black and white. There are the good and the bad, and resolution is achieved through conflict. C, M and V live in different worlds and draw on different story forms or genres to interpret their experiences of loss and conflict. V synthesizes the information from a number of supportive relationships to create an enabling story. M is confronted with a situation he cannot resolve but arrives at a conclusion which, while not being realistic, at least places the problem in the future. C, empowered by the belief that he can overcome or at least survive conflict, sees bereavement as another battle to be fought in the future.

However, while V can be optimistic, M is not, and C is already experiencing the difficulties that arise from adopting a conflictual attitude to the needs and demands of others in a social situation. This is progressively disruptive of his progress in school and eventually proves impossible to deal with.

Significantly it would seem, we asked to interview the parents of all three children, but only V's mother was willing to participate.

One of the tentative conclusions drawn from these interviews was that children relate the world of their experience in different ways in accordance with the relationships established with those with whom they are closely involved, most obviously in the home environment. On the basis of this, they evaluate what is offered to them at school in the way of learning, most obviously in the pattern of participation or otherwise that is nurtured in their home situation. What cannot be positively addressed at home is unlikely to be positively facilitated at school to any great degree. Attitudes then become the key issue to address in considering the development of children. Elsewhere we have used the concept of 'genre' in children's storying to analyse this issue in greater depth.

B

B was first interviewed in a group of four children using the poem 'Looking for Dad'. In this group, three children responded by saying that they missed their dad (with these children their fathers had left home and they had stayed with their mothers) and two by expressing concern over the illness of a grandparent or younger brother. B had responded in both respects.

T, B and H's responses provided the most graphic explanation of events:

Q: How's the little boy feeling?
T: Sad.
Q: Do you ever feel sad like that?
T: Yes, because my dad's just left home. He was fighting. Daddy was living at another house. I went there and Daddy never brought me back and that's why they went to court [mum and dad]. Now we don't know where Daddy lives; Daddy knows where we live, Daddy's mum has got the phone number and I went and slept at Daddy's mummy's house.
Q: Did you enjoy that?
T: Yes, it was in Leicester.
Q: But you haven't seen your dad?
T: No.
Q: Do you miss him?
T: Yes.
Q: B, is there anyone you miss?
B: My dad.
T: Everyone misses their dad.
Q: Where is your dad?
B: My mum married because he is too busy, someone I know about. I've another dad called S. My mum and dad fight. I live with mum and S cos my dad chucked

> my mum on the floor head first.

T: My baby brother was born about that big [*small*]. He still goes to hospital.

Q: How old is he? Is he new?

T: One and he can't walk ... he can stand up and clap. We've got a picture about him that's really sad.

H: My aunty ... (*indistinct*)

Q: Do you ever wonder where's she gone or speak to her in your head?

H: No, you just cry – often.

Q. What do you think when you cry?

H: I just wish she was still there.

The children ended the interview by giving a message to someone they loved.

Q: Say one last thing into the tape. If there's one last person who you'd like to give a message to because you miss them would you just think who it might be?

B: My brother.

T: How can I because she's up in heaven?

Q: That's OK, you can still give the message.

T: How?

N: She can hear you, can't you throw it up in the air? She can hear you, can't she? (*To me*)

B: I know what to say now. See you soon R because I know your mum and grandma's ill and I just hope she gets well so you can come down [from Scotland].

N: I know what to say now. I hope you get well grandad.

T: I hope I see my daddy again.

H: I hope that I see my aunty again.

B was then interviewed with K. On this occasion we went for a walk on the estate. They were asked to take me to their favourite places. Two of B's favourite places were the playground on the estate and a waste dump at the back of the park. In the playground he goes on the swings.

B's story

The estate is fine because there is a playground, trees to climb and thousands of mates to play with. Not all my friends live on the estate. My brother doesn't, he lives up in Scotland. I've got a long way to go and see him, I normally see him twice a year in Scotland.

I like playing on the swings in the park. It feels like a rocket going backwards and forwards up on the air. I like playing on the trees as well. The swings are different if you shut your eyes. If you shut your eyes on the swing it feels scary. It's black and it looks like you're in space. Sometimes it feels like I'm going to Scotland on my swing – whoosh! And then when I get to Scotland I'm going to look for my brother.

When I'm in a special place I like to think of special people, even though they're not there, like I think of my brother in Scotland, even though he's not here.

I miss my dad. My mum married again because he's too busy with someone. I've another dad called S. My mum and dad fight. I live with my mum and S cos my dad chucked my mum on the floor head first.

Later, at the dump, B creates a boat from various detritus: wooden pallets, a spin-dryer, washing machine, etc. On the boat he repeats that we are going to Scotland to see his brother.

Significant features of these places of play lie in children's ability to use them as locations where they can release their minds from everyday concerns and dwell on underlying, personal issues. In this respect they are no different from adults. Once the imagination is released by the creation of mental and spiritual space the world opens up and new horizons appear, peopled by those who lie in our memories. B uses what is available to him in the playground and park to stir these memories into life and to remain in touch with the brother from whom he is separated.

Similarly, K regards the playground as a space where she can recall those who are and have been important to her: 'I think of all the family, the people who's died as well. Like my grandad and nan what's died as well.'

In this respect these environments are also places of memorial and remembrance where significant relationships are relived and rejoined, but not necessarily resolved.

Conclusions

Carrying out this first phase of our research confirmed a number of expectations but also taught us much more.

- We expected that children would have stories to tell about what interested them, but we were surprised at the number of children who communicated deep-seated hopes, fears and concerns about their experiences.
- We expected that some children would have had disturbing experiences which they wrestled with but not that a large percentage of the class we interviewed would be dealing with lives fragmented by loss and conflict.
- We expected that children might refer to significant events which caused them some distress but not that they would trust outsiders with powerful and secret stories which were very private to them.
- We did not expect that we would find children of this age had already developed quite complex explanations of their experiences with reference to enabling concepts onto which they had placed their own interpretations.
- We did not expect that their imaginations would be used to such serious purpose in coping with difficulties arising through loss and separation.
- We had not realized the value of the role played by adults close to them who had facilitated the development of their explanations or the significance for children of not having adults who fulfilled this role.
- We had not realized the unfulfilled need that some children have to talk through their experiences with an adult who is separate from the circumstances and people with whom they are usually involved.
- We were not aware of how willing children would be to talk with other children who shared similar experiences and concerns.

- We were surprised by the way in which these children could construct or utilize metaphorical language consciously or unconsciously in order to explain what would otherwise have been incommunicable.
- We became aware that image and symbol, ritual and play were of great importance in the way that children constructed and maintained the most important aspects of their worldviews by enabling them to stay in touch with those whom they missed or were absent from.

The results of this research led us to explore this theme further in another school. This is the subject of Chapter 7.

References

Patten, B. (1985) Looking for Dad. *Gargling with Jelly.* London, Puffin.

5 Children's religious and scientific thinking

Jane Erricker

Introduction

In our society today, in our homes and in our schools, we do not really listen to what children have to say. This simple statement is one that has permeated this book so far and will continue to do so in this chapter. It is an interesting statement because, as teachers, we are trained to listen to children. It is a major part of our job. We are trained to listen because we should begin our teaching 'where the children are', and because we do our assessment at least partly by listening to what children repeat back to us after a lesson. But our listening is tightly linked to an agenda of our own. In other words, we have already worked out what we want to hear from the children, and we can recognize when it is or is not there, but we do not hear anything outside of those parameters. It is like listening to a child calling for its mother – you don't hear the birds sing. We want to find out how much the children know about a curriculum area before we start teaching it, and we want to know how much they have learned when we have finished teaching it. In the present climate of teaching, with a very crowded curriculum, we simply do not have time to allow children to talk 'off task'.

In this chapter I am going to describe some conversations with 6-year-old children. When I was doing this work I followed the methodology described earlier in this book in that I tried to ask very open-ended questions and follow the leads that the children gave me. I was probably less open-ended than some of the other researchers because I wanted to give the children an opportunity to talk about science in some way and therefore I tended to nudge the conversations in a particular direction through my questioning. I was very surprised by the depth of the children's thinking, and by the sophistication of their arguments. When I left the children I asked myself why I was surprised. Why did I expect the children to be less able than was actually demonstrated by their conversation? What had led to my having the expectations that I took into the research situation?

I realized that I believed that children are not able to think and argue in this way because I believed they are not experienced enough and because they are somehow not clever enough. I am sure that this latter belief of mine owes a great deal to the work of psychologists such as Piaget, whose ideas of developmental stages allow us to make general judgements about the abilities of children of certain ages. Children of only 6 years old are judged not to be at the developmental stage that allows them to think in the abstract as I believe my children were doing. These ideas have been challenged by more recent researchers such as Margaret Donaldson of course, but the legacy of Piaget's work obviously remains in my consciousness and results in my underestimating the children.

The idea of lack of life experience is also spurious. Children today, especially those living in difficult economic and social circumstances, have had a great deal of life experience, even by the age of 6. For our own comfort, we adults like to think that these experiences do not impinge on children's consciousness too much, that they are too young to understand. This allows us to be more at ease with our own shortcomings because we have difficulty in admitting them to children, and in dealing with them. One important lesson our research has taught us is that this is not the case, and that these experiences impinge very strongly on children. The problem is that this comforting belief results in inadequate provision for children in helping them to deal with difficult existential problems. This issue is dealt with in more detail later in this book.

The children whom I talked to were prepared to discuss and argue with me and each other about issues of moral importance. These issues could not be resolved, because they are irresolvable by anyone, whether child or adult, philosopher or theologian, but these children tried very hard to do so. Their arguments were logical, they supported their opinions by quoting authority, and they illustrated their points with examples from their own life experiences. It may be possible to claim that two of these children were particularly intelligent, and they certainly were very bright, but I don't think they were exceptional. I just think I gave them the time and the opportunity.

The research

This chapter relates the stories told by these children in an inner city school when they were asked questions about things that are important to them in their lives. Five children were actually interviewed, but this chapter largely concentrates on two of them. They were Year 2 children, interviewed during the autumn term when they were nearly 7 years old. They were selected by the headteacher of the school as being articulate and sociable children, who would be willing, even eager, to talk to me. They were not selected because they were thought to be particularly able, though I certainly gained a high opinion of their intelligence during the interviews. The school selected itself, in that the headteacher had heard about our research project and expressed a desire to be involved. She felt that her children would be interesting and, more important, that the children would benefit from the extra one-to-one attention they would receive. The feeling that, as a researcher, I was welcomed and valued as a contributor to the children's well-being affected my attitude very positively and resulted in relaxed, enjoyable and productive interviews.

I interviewed the children in the school library, and in the resource room when the library was being used. Both of these environments were suitable in that we were away from the disturbances of other children, but unsuitable in that they were full of potential distractions. The children tried to answer some of my questions by finding relevant books, or occasionally tried to avoid answering the questions by finding things to play with.

The children

The children I spoke to were R, L, J, N and A. They were not all in the same class. Although I will recount conversations that involved all five children I will concentrate on N and A. It will help you to put their opinions into context if I tell you a little about each child.

N was 6 years old, almost 7. He was an extremely attractive black child who came from Malawi. He lived with his mother and at the time of the interviews also had an aunty from Indonesia staying with the family. He had a 29-year-old brother living in Malawi. N was very lively and talkative, and did not like staying in one place for any length of time. He had strong opinions which he was not afraid to voice, and these influenced the other children in the group.

A was also 6 years old. He was very concerned that his name should be pronounced correctly, and was rather contemptuous of anyone who got it wrong. He was confident and reflective. His parents were separated but he went to see his father regularly.

Both children attended church: N the Evangelical church and A the local Anglican church.

R and L are twins, both 6 years old, with a younger sister of 3. The family had several pets, and during the course of my contact with the children some of them died, were killed or given away. Neither child had had any specifically religious nurture.

J was very chatty and giggly. She made jokes and throwaway comments while the other children were talking. She has a baby brother and a father who had been in a motorbike accident a short while before the interviews. I was told by the teachers at the school that J had been alone with her grandmother when she died, and had covered her with a blanket until someone else came home. There was no evidence of any religious nurture.

The conversations

My discussions with these children centred around two specific areas: death and heaven, and the killing of animals. In both of these areas it was interesting to observe the children combining information that they had been given in a scientific context and in the context of religious education or at church. There was no overt conflict between these two sources and no sense that one source had more credibility than the other. They used whichever seemed most appropriate, given the experiences that they had had, and the source or sources to which they had been given access by their education and their nurture. The following extracts illustrate their thinking. In all of them Q indicates a question or statement from me.

Death and heaven

The ideas that the children had about death and what happened after death drew on their scientific knowledge and on their religious concepts, but also, in J's case, on neither of these two. J's concerns revolved around her family, and she did not often enter the conversation at a more general level. When we were discussing the death of pets she did not believe, as some of the others did, that they went to heaven. She thought that

> They've faded away.
> They just stay there.... In the ground if you bury them.
> If I did bury it I'd make sure it went away. I don't like dead rabbits in my garden.
> ... throw 'em in the dustbin.

Her views may have been influenced by science work on decay that the class had been doing, but she had quite negative and cynical views on the whole subject of religion, expressed by 'jokes' and throw-away comments when the others spoke of anything to do with religious concepts. Also, although I hesitate to draw this kind of conclusion on such a limited amount of dialogue with J, she may be expressing an anger with the whole idea of death because of her experiences with her grandmother. Her recent and very real experience of death combined with her scientific knowledge could have led her to a position which appears pessimistic compared to other, much more comfortable views of pets in heaven. Her picture of heaven showed stars and clouds, but the people in heaven would be 'just lying dead like that'.

R and L were both at home with scientific concepts in answering my questions about the state of the world and the existence of something after death. L accepted the death of pets in a matter-of-fact way, and explained to me why it was important that we kept trees alive: 'if there were no trees we wouldn't have no oxygen.'

R had his own ideas about the nature of heaven, which he described as another planet.

Q: Whose heaven?
R: The animals, up in the sky. In the stars and planets.

He believed that 'We don't go up to heaven when we're buried but when animals are buried they go up to heaven'.

He sees God in heaven looking after everyone just like a doctor, and wearing green clothes. He drew a picture of his idea of heaven, which was a planet with holes from which aliens emerged to collect the animals when they died. R did not think that every animal which died went to heaven. L helped him to explain to me that if you flushed an animal like a goldfish down the lavatory, they could not go to heaven because their body was not able to 'float up'. Thus they did not have a concept of souls or spirits which went to heaven.

R and L's view on the issues of death and heaven are very fluid. They are influenced by the views of N and A which are strongly expressed, with the stamp of religious authority, as I will demonstrate later, but are rooted in scientific ideas of earth, space and ecology. N talked about his dog which had died and was in heaven. He went on to say that everything in the world came from heaven and that God made all of us and has told us, in the Bible, to look after the world. He is so sure of the authority of the Bible that he tries to quote chapter and verse to support his statements.

Q: Have you read in the Bible that we have to look after the world, N?

N: I was ... one says that ... I forget it ... it's chapter 16 verse 5.

Q: Where in the Bible, N?

N: Chapter 5 verse 5 ... chapter 15 verse 5.

Q: And it tells us we have to look after the world, does it?

N: I'm talking about another verse this time.

He shows he is aware that in order to make his story convincing he has to indicate his sources. He and the other children have a conversation together which begins with N showing off.

N: I know why God's a miracle.

Q: Why?

N: Because he made himself ... He made himself out of nothing. And he made us out of soil.

L: I think Jesus made the world.

N: Jesus made the world! No, he didn't!

A: No, he was born after the world was made.

N has very consistent views about God and Jesus which fit in with Christian ideas. He is prepared to tackle difficult issues, such as who made God if God made the world, and has his own explanation that God is a miracle because he made himself. He is prepared to try to fit together Christian ideas and scientific concepts.

N: Space is really big and when space is ending then on top of space is heaven.

N thinks that people go to heaven when they die, and that

heaven is full of spirits. He says that spirits are like ghosts, but he does not think there are ghosts in heaven. When I asked him to draw me a picture of heaven he drew me a picture of a house. I naively asked him whether this was what he thought heaven was like and he told me that heaven was full of spirits and they are just thin air, and as you cannot draw thin air, so he had drawn me a house. He labelled it heaven just to keep me happy. This is the clearest indication I have ever had that it is very unwise to try to interpret children's drawings without entering into a dialogue with the artist to establish what the drawing means. I certainly would have got this one wrong. What children say when they have drawn a picture not only describes what they have drawn, but also what they meant to draw, and what thinking there was behind the drawing. This is not to say that the exercise of doing the drawing is not necessary, rather that it acts as a conduit for their ideas.

When I asked A what heaven was like he said: 'That's a good question. None of us know that.' However, he did know that God lived there, and when he drew heaven he drew it populated with skeletons: 'I think all the people are skeletons and God is not.'

Out of these five children, it was only those with specifically religious nurture, N and A, who had a concept of heaven as a place where we go after death, or any idea of the nature of the entity, body or soul, that they believed went to heaven. R was able to produce an idea based on his knowledge of earth and space but I do not think he had ever thought about the issue before we talked. In the light of the work we have done with other children, for example, in Chapter 4, it is interesting to ask whether some kind of consideration of what happens after death, be it based on a specific faith or not, is helpful to a child when dealing with bereavement. It seems to me, as a result of my conversations, that unless the issue is raised within the context of religious commitment, it is not raised at all with children of this age. R had obviously tried to construct a picture based on scientific ideas, but it lacked conviction or real meaning to him, concentrating as it did on the fate of animals after death. It seems likely that some kind of discussion of the issue, without necessarily confining it to one faith or another but considering a range of possibilities, would give children some concepts to draw upon when they lose someone whom they love.

Killing animals

This issue was debated mainly by N and A, in response to my initial questions about why we should look after the world. I was hoping to open up an area where they could use religious and scientific reasons for their answers and as usual the children took the discussion in their own direction. I asked why we should look after animals. A replied:

> A: Because very nasty people are trying to kill them.
> Q: Are they? Why?
> A: Because they want to eat them.

He was beginning to realize that there might be a problem here.

> Q: And you don't think people should kill animals to eat them?
> A: Cos their mummies will ... kill the person.

R felt it was necessary to kill animals so that we could eat meat; otherwise we would die. A knew that we get meat from animals, but he was still not happy about killing them, even if they were in the jungle and going to hurt him. He was concerned with the issue of conservation.

> Q: You think it's OK to kill animals in the jungle.
> A: No, it's not cos that's how we get less animals in the jungle.
> Q: It's OK to kill animals if they're going to hurt you?
> A: I'm not sure about that.

N, on the other hand, had a very pragmatic approach to the problem, explained with reference to an imaginary situation, but possibly one he had experienced, at least anecdotally, in

Malawi before he moved to Britain.

> N: What I mean about it is when you go in the jungle to see lions ... you see elephants, you see snakes.
>
> Q: And do you think it's OK to kill those animals?
>
> N: Yeah. If they're ... Because if you are going into the jungle and you knew the way to go out and you saw a lion and you ran and you imagine there was a stone on the ground and you tripped on it and they could bite you.
>
> Q: So is it OK to kill animals if they're going to hurt you?
>
> N: Yes.

The whole question of killing animals for food is returned to in the next interview that I had with these two children, N and A.

> Q: Why should we look after animals?
>
> A: Cos they're God's animals ... And they should produce more babies and they shouldn't, they should have loads of species.
>
> N: And have a happy time.
>
> Q: And have a happy time. And A thinks there ought to be lots of species. What's a species, A?
>
> A: Lots of different kinds of animals.
>
> Q: Why do you want there to be lots of different kinds of animals?
>
> A: So we can carry on getting more and more.
>
> Q: What would happen if we didn't have more and more animals?
>
> A: They, they'd, they can be extinct.
>
> Q: They'd be extinct. Would that be a bad thing?
>
> A and N: Yes.
>
> Q: Why? Why would it be a bad thing?
>
> A: Because God wants to have animals on his land.
>
> Q: God wants to have animals on his land. Is that how you feel too, N?
>
> N: Yes, and if he um, if he um, if he ... it's like if you kill

71

God's animals then he'll be very sad and upset. It's just like you've just bought a very nice toy which you have had, and then the next day somebody comes and breaks it all up.

A: That's what it's like.

Q: Why does he think they're precious?

N: If you make something out of paper and then it all burns up, would you be sad?

Q: Yes, that's right, you'd be sad, wouldn't you?

N: You'd make those animals sad if you killed them and he'd be sad because he'd have to make some more.

A: They kill whales to get oil from whales.

Q: They do. What do you think about that?

A: It's not really fair for the whales or the animals because people get to kill them and then they get to eat them or use them for something and the animals should live.

N: And then the people use the oil for lighting up lamps.

Q: What about food? Do you eat burgers and things?

A and N: Yes.

A: Animals, farm animals are OK because they produce pork and they have loads of babies.

Q: So is it OK to eat an animal if they produce loads of babies?

N: Yes, because there'll be some more left.

A: You don't have to kill a mummy cow for milk, do you?

Q: No, that's right, you can get milk without killing the mummy cow.

N: Yes, I know why you can buy pigs, farmers get pigs and then some people want them to sell meat, to sell pork with them and that's all right because they'll have babies and they have eaten fresh food and healthy food because … if you buy it from the wild, then you'd have to be careful, that there're no bad bits.

Q: Yes. Does God mind us killing animals for food?

N: Yes.

Q: He does.

N: Some of them.

Q: Right. Does he mind us killing pigs for pork and cows for burgers?

N: I don't know.

A: I think that's why he put them on there ... not the wild animals.

Q: Do you think that God thinks we're more important than animals?

A: Animals are more important.

Q: Animals are more important?

A: No, they're both the same cos God likes us all the same.

N: He likes us all.

A: We're not just ... we're not important, we're not very important.

N: It's very important ... the things that he made.

A: Animals are very important for people because they ... the land as well.

Q: Because they look after the land.

A: You see cos we don't have ... if we only had ... if we had people today and no animals the sea would be ... it would completely be gone.

Q: The sea would be gone?

A: No.

Q: The land ...?

A: Nothing would be ... only fish would be in the sea.

N: We won't have any food.

Q: Right.

N: We won't have any food from the animals.

Q: No we wouldn't if all the animals were gone.

A: Cos people love killing.

Q: Do they?

N: Some of them do.

Q: Do you think people love killing?

A: Yes.

N: I think some. Some of them don't.

A: But they kill things cos they like it.

N: Course they don't. Some of them might have said that um ... why don't we leave ... if it's a big why don't we

> leave ... if it's too young why don't we leave ... if it's too young why don't we leave this for just a bit more while to grow big.
>
> Q: And then kill them?
>
> N: No, when it's ...
>
> A: Let them die or ... let them die.
>
> N: If you want to kill them ... not want to eat them, you just want to kill them and you don't want to sell them for things to eat then you should just kill them when they're ill.
>
> Q: Apart from that you shouldn't kill?
>
> N: Yes.
>
> Q: What about you A? How do you know you shouldn't kill?
>
> A: Because God tells us not to.
>
> Q: Has God actually told you? Has he actually spoken to you?
>
> A and N: Yes.
>
> N: He speaks to you in the Bible.

It is interesting to follow the way the children construct their arguments, the authority they base their opinions on, and the way in which both my questions, and the opinions that they express to each other, make them alter their positions slightly.

A starts by using God as his authority for not killing animals, but quickly moves to a position based on his knowledge of conservation issues, that is, we must not make species extinct. However, when asked the difficult question, why not, he returns to God as the reason. N backs up A's argument by using his own experience to explain how God feels when animals are killed. He is at great pains to ensure that I understand how upset God would be. A is concerned about the justice of depriving animals of life so that people can obtain something useful, but I then confronted them with the issue of killing animals for meat, which they both eat. I was interested to see how they would argue here, with their opinions and their actions in conflict. Both used the argument that there were plenty of farm animals; in other words, they were not endangered species, and therefore it was allowable to kill them for meat. A was obviously still unhappy with this because he asked if you have to kill a cow to get milk. Both were sure that God does not like us killing animals, but A decided that God put farm animals there for us to eat. They returned to the idea that animals are somehow necessary for the whole natural world to work properly and that we would not have enough food if all the animals were gone. A, very seriously and with the air of someone who has just realized a very unpleasant truth, said that people love killing. N found it very difficult to accept this and tried to justify his position, which involves allowing people to kill old and ill animals.

To summarize their argument, we should not kill animals

- because God says we must not and it would make him unhappy since the world belongs to Him and He made it;
- but He makes an exception in the case of farm animals because we need to eat them;
- because they are endangered species;
- because they are necessary for the ecology of the planet;
- because it is wrong to kill something just for gain;
- unless it is in self-defence.

These arguments are

1. theological, citing God as the authority to justify the opinions;
2. scientific, citing scientific ideas as justification;
3. they come from an innate sense of what is right and wrong – what is fair – without any authority being cited.

Within the limitations of their vocabulary and experience, these children used a full range of arguments to justify their opinions about the issues under discussion. The arguments ranged across all the categories in Kohlberg's stage analysis of moral development, even though the children were only 6 years old and Kohlberg's research included children of up to 14 years old. As I said in the introduction to this chapter, these children were very bright, but not exceptionally so, suggesting that many children could think at this level if only given the opportunity to do so.

References

Kohlberg, L. (1981) *The Philosophy of Moral Development.* San Francisco, Harper & Row.

6 The identity of 'Asian' children

Cathy Ota

Making contact with the school

A colleague at work suggested making contact with this school because of its rich ethnic mix. Our initial meeting with the headteacher, in June 1994, was a valuable starting point. The headteacher described the school and the community of which it was a part, as well as the different ways in which the school was addressing issues concerning the developing identity of the children.

The school serves three main communities which live together in a small area described by the headteacher as 'a contained and encapsulated world'. The Sikh community is the largest group in the area and the second largest is the Pakistani Muslims. The newest arrivals to the area are the Bengali Muslims.

Our research appeared to fit in well with how the school saw its role in empowering the children and affirming their identity and we arranged to begin interviews with small groups from Years 4 and 5. We decided to make the groups mixed gender and mixed community and to talk to them about general issues which they felt affected them, speaking from their own experience.

Interviews

We managed to interview 23 children during the rest of the summer term, ten from Year 4 and thirteen from Year 5. From these, two boys and two girls from Year 5 were interviewed a second time. In the autumn term of 1994 ten children were interviewed from Years 4 and 5 and we also talked to fifteen children from Year 3. We returned to re-interview two boys and two girls from Year 3 in June 1995. In total, 43 children were interviewed and of this group eight were interviewed a second time. The children were very confident and friendly and most responded well to the chance to sit down to talk about themselves and what was important to them. At first we interviewed in groups of four or five, but we discovered it was difficult to allow everyone the chance to talk as much as they wanted. On top of this, transcribing the tapes was almost impossible with five children all trying to talk at once! As the autumn term progressed we looked at other ways of conducting the interviews; groups of five were too large and certain 'principles' had emerged:

- We realized that the girls felt more comfortable with me and that the boys enjoyed talking to Clive, so we started to work separately with pairs of boys and girls. This encouraged the children, particularly the girls, to speak more freely.
- We followed what the child talked about, the concepts and terms they introduced and let them unpack their meanings. This presented problems in that it meant trusting the children to come up with the goods rather than pushing them into a discussion about what you the interviewer thought was important or particularly relevant.

After introducing ourselves to the children we asked the initial question 'What's it like living round here?' This stimulated a discussion which raised many issues and areas to explore with them. We also used drawing as a way of focusing the interview and providing something for us to talk about in greater depth. Several topics cropped up often in the conversations. All the children talked about their families; this included parents, siblings, grandparents, cousins, uncles and aunts, whether they lived in the same house, same street, in other parts of Britain, India, Bangladesh or Pakistan. Another topic was the role of religion in their lives: culturally, socially and as a framework for behaviour and addressing existential concerns.

Much of what was discussed concerned the attempts of the children to establish their own identity within the different worlds they inhabited. Many drew on well-defined guidelines provided by their family and local community, but there was also evidence of them trying to take account of other experiences and environments such as school, what they saw on television, and, for the older ones, the prospect of moving on to secondary school.

From our interviews it seems that two major elements contribute to the identity of the children – gender and ethnicity. Both have a dramatic effect on the way the children perceive themselves and others around them and it is these two areas I wish to examine in the rest of this chapter.

Ethnicity

W, a boy in Year 5, shows how many of the children expressed their ethnicity;

W: I like this school cos there's a lot of Asians and a lot of my cousins in this school ... I've got a lot of cousins round this area and a lot of friends ... there's a lot of Asians round this area as well.

Q: Are you all the same religion?

W: No.

Q: Can you tell me something about that?

S: Yes, me and G are Sikhs and them both are Muslims, I don't know what, are you Bengali? (*To N*) She's Bengali.

W: Yes, Muslims are quite the same thing here ... both religions believe in the same God, Allah.

Q: Right, and you're Bengali (*to N*) and W?

W: Muslim.

Q: And are you Bengali?

W: Pakistani ... like there be some Muslims and different Muslims as well ... we're different Muslims that do believe in our own prophet.

Q: Right, so you have your own mosque too?

W: Yes, she goes to this Bengali mosque but they teach the same thing ... they appreciate it there more, more comfortable there cos there's a lot of Bengal there.

W illustrates how:

- the children referred to themselves as Asian;
- after further discussion they identified themselves in terms of a distinct ethnic group;
- the religious and cultural group was an important aspect of their position in school;
- they were all very aware of the importance of each other's background.

The children also showed considerable understanding of the beliefs and differences between other groups and their own:

D: I want to talk about their religion and about God ... you know their God, he thinks that, you know the Muslim people in it, they have food and then some people, they leave their food and then throw it in the bin and you know God says that, you know that people that have no food, you lot throw food away, you take food for granted. That's why they do the, what's it called?

O: Fasting.

D: Yes.

Q: Is that right? Do you want to say something back?

O: Yes, sometimes that's right, but we have to sometimes think of poor people.

D: That's what I'm trying to say.

In a similar way to their use of the generic term 'Asian', the children used the term 'Indian' to describe themselves and their religion:

F: I go to Indian school too and read the Indian, about er, so I can see what's God doing.

In one interview I asked S to draw something special:

S: Our church?

Q: Yes? Why would you like to draw a picture of your church?

S: I don't know, it just came into my head.

Q: You like your church do you?

S: Yes.

Q: And what do you do when you go to the church?

S: First we take our shoes off, we go upstairs, and then we pray and we come downstairs, then we sit down and have our dinner and then we go outside and play.

Q: Right, so what sort of prayers do you say?

S: There's like Indian prayers, I like all my churches.

Q: So what religion are you?

S: Indian.

Q: Indian?

S: Yes.

What is interesting is the language used by the children, identifying themselves primarily as Asian or Indian, and then as Muslim, Sikh, Pakistani or Bengali. Of course, part of this may be a response to talking with us – white interviewers asking basic questions about their lives. Even if this is the case we can see how they want to identify themselves as Asian and Indian in order to differentiate themselves from the white person they find themselves talking to. The school encourages integration and mixing, in terms of both gender and ethnicity, aiming to facilitate an identity as members of a whole mixed community rather than just a separate group. The school uses several practical measures to encourage this, such as seating the children alternately boy, girl, boy, girl in assembly. During our interviews we could see how the school had overcome tensions connected with the children's background or roles as defined for them by their community and religious adherence. D and S, Sikh and Muslim boys respectively, are just one example of this:

S: I can do bhangra dancing, it's from India. It's about the farmer working at harvest time, you wave your hands around and jump up and down squatting on your legs.

D: And reggae dancing. We mixed the reggae and bhangra dancing together and changed it to make it more exciting. We start off with the bhangra music because it's got like a lot of kind of Indian words in it and then we started dancing backwards and forwards with some reggae. There's a boy in class 6 who sings along in Punjabi and Urdu. Then he changes into reggae songs.

We practise and Sir gives us some of the timetable to practise. We've done some concerts, we went to the secondary school and did one. We also did one in the first school and at the nursery.

S: It's really exciting doing the dancing, it's like spreading out like, instead of curling up.

D: It makes you easy and relaxed. It's like getting free, free, free like to do what you want and not letting other people control your life so that you can do things with your mates, for once.

From this we can see how much the opportunity and experience of dancing means to the boys, how they value and recognize its importance in their lives for a number of reasons:

- they are able to make decisions about how they dance;
- they have performed concerts to different groups who have enjoyed watching them;
- it is something they do for their own enjoyment and satisfaction;
- they recognize the experience of liberation and freedom it provides.

However, the differences between the Muslim and Sikh children also caused tension and our research uncovered undercurrents of conflict between children of different religious and ethnic backgrounds:

Z: There's lots of different people here, there's Pakistani people, there's Hindi people, Indian people, Bengali people.

Q: What makes them so different?

Z: Because if they're Indian they always listen to the bad angel, not the good one.

Q: Why's that?

Z: Because they don't like Muslim people, some of them.

Q: And are people in this school like that?

Z: Yeh.

Y: Some are different, sometimes the Indian people do listen to the good angels, sometimes, but not all the time.

These conversations illustrate several aspects of the children's lives:

- They show the tensions arising from the sense of identity and role given to the children within their different habitats.
- Their *religious community* provides a strong sense of identity in terms of religious and cultural heritage.
- The *school* provides a different message of integration and mixing together.
- The *home environment* appears to operate between the two, supporting both the community and school in varying degrees.

We can see this in the way the children express different ambitions. When talking about themselves as adults, the fundamental role of gender is noticeable in constructing their identity and worldviews.

Gender

D (Sikh) and S (Muslim), whom we have already met, spoke about their ambitions for the future:

S: My dad wants me to work, get a good job ... I think about working ... being a house drawer, design houses. I hope I do that and have a big company and all that, I want to be a businessman.

D: If I become a footballer I'm going to buy a massive, a 32-storey company in New York ... and when the [football] season's over, I'm going go down and fly out to

> New York, and control my business there and if I'm not
> there, I'm going to let my, my secretary take over, or my
> wife.

D's comment about his wife is indicative of how the girls
perceived their role in the future. Many spoke about leaving
home and looking after their husband's family. Z and Y, 7-
year-old girls, had a more traditional image of what would
happen when they grew up:

> Y: I don't want to get married because when you're little
> you can go to the shops on your own and that, but when
> you're grown up you can't.
>
> Z: You have to get married, if you don't listen to your dad
> or mum they would hit you and then they have to lock
> you up in this room and you're not allowed to have
> nothing to eat and that's why you have to get married
> and you have to listen to your parents ... But when you
> marry, the person they marry, they have to leave their
> mum and dad and go to the boy's mum and dad, you
> have to leave your mum and dad and your sisters and
> brothers.
>
> Q: Do you think that would be difficult?
>
> Z: Yeh and you have to leave but you're not allowed to go
> to their house and back again, you stay in the boy's
> house.
>
> Q: So how do you feel about doing that sort of thing?
>
> Z: I wish I can't but you *have* to do that.

Z later spoke about wanting to have a shop when she was
older:

> Z: The boy has to tell you which shop you can open and
> if he say no shop then you have to stay home and clean
> the house.

Older girls had different ambitions, even though they still
acknowledged that their role was to look after a husband and
family, as Y and H, two 9-year-olds, show:

H: Do you know, when that person is married, they have to go to the boy's house and you know the boy's parents, you have to do some work like for them.

Q: Do you think that might be difficult?

H: Yes, cos we miss our mum and dad.

Q: Is there anything else you'd like to do when you're older?

H: I want to work actually, be a nurse or something.

Y: I want to be a airport girl, when you're one of the luggage girls.

Q: Would you be able to be a nurse do you think, H?

H: Yes, cos my cousin's a nurse ... but when I get married I would stay at home or something.

Y: I'd still do a job cos we don't really mind that much.

Staff in the school spoke about how the influence of religious leaders was perhaps not so great as it had been and that parents had aspirations for both their sons and daughters:

'The parents I've spoken to, they're saying "yes, we want them to have a university education if they're capable of it".'

'Ten years ago they would say our daughters can't go on to education, they're with us and staying home. I had one incident when my eldest daughter was Year 7 or 8, and one teacher turned around and says to me "Oh it's not worth bothering with Asian girls because they end up in the kitchen" and I was really angry about that.'

'They are saying "we were deprived of a good education" ... so they want these things for the kids and I sort of emphasize that ... life is hard enough if you've got a good education, let alone if you haven't ... so they're really keen for the girls to get on ... I think now that it won't really be a conflict between the home and the school because the home wants that as well.'

These graphic examples show how the girls' identity in the present is forcibly shaped by their perceived roles in the future.

85

We also found that the way in which boys and girls relate to each other is affected:

Y: You know like in India right, in every Indian religion they don't like girls that much.
Q: What happens in England?
Y: Down here they think that they are the same, that boys and the girls are the same ... but some men who come from India, they don't like girls, they say like do this, do that, use us as their slave and that ... because you know like a girl, it's not really fair on girls cos they have to do all the housework, why not boys and that? So if you treated them the same that would be better.

Y's comments that boys should do some housework are unlikely to be heeded; many of the girls spoke of the work they had to do in the home, often while the boys had the freedom to go out as they pleased and play:

A: Girls are the best cos the girls do work for their mothers.
Q: What do the boys do then?
A: Nothing, they just play out.
H: Yeh, boys play computer.

It is probably difficult to overestimate the influence of gender in the development of identity for the girls. For example, many girls recognized that boys were far more preferable in families to girls:

S: We got a baby boy and he be really special.
Q: Why's that?
L: Cos everybody likes a baby boy and there should only be one girl in the family cos you need boys.
Q: So what happens if you have more than one girl in the family?
L: It's bad news but like you still get some money ... they get sad because they got girls, the girls are not as good as boys ... my mum wishes she had a boy.
S: We're happy now we got a baby boy.

S and L were more positive about India and being a girl there, but this may have had more to do with receiving attention and presents than a general attitude to girls:

L: At India they respect ...
Q: They respect you?
L: Yeh.
Q: They don't respect you over here?
L: No.
Q: Why not?
S: Because they don't like us and at India they pick us up and take us to the shops and get us some sweets and they get us balls and things like that ... they share more things at India ... I said to my mum, my aunty came on Saturday, from India, I said to my mum 'why can't I go there cos they respects me, cos only in India they respects me'.
Q: What does it mean if someone respects you?
S: Like, they care about us.

Although positive about India, the girls discussed an undercurrent of tension and conflict between the boys and girls in school:

Q: How do boys treat you? Are they nice to you?
S: Like they're nasty to us sometimes ... sometimes the boys hit us ... sometimes they say 'your mum's gonna get dead, your dad's gonna get dead' ... sometimes they say bad things to our mum and dad.
L: In Indian, and I don't know what they say.
S: They speak in Indian.
L: We've got lots of Indian people in our class.
Q: Is that good?
L: No, cos they swear ... there shouldn't be much boys, there should only be girls, there should be like in 3T like all of the boys, like all of the boys in one class.
Q: Right, and all the girls in the other?
L: Yeh.

Q: Why would that be better?

L: Cos they can't swear at us.

As a result of this interview I met with the headteacher and steps were immediately taken to deal with the swearing, even though it was indicative of the general way women and girls were often regarded by boys and men in their communities, and consequently difficult to overcome completely. Even so, the head was keen to take action:

'I think you have to talk to the kids about it, you know, as a whole, and then get them to come up with their solutions, like each time they're sworn at, if they just put their hand up, don't say anything … I mean the best thing is to get them to stop of their own accord, rather than enforce it. But I think it's important that we make our position clear to the kids that it's not on.'

'If it's a low level thing that's going on all the time, it almost sounds as if it's accepted … it used to be a lot more overt in the school, there was a lot of physical violence towards girls, that's all stopped. But we've still got these other layers of the onion to peel off and even if they do carry on … back in their community, they've got to be able to transfer and they can't go up to a secondary school or a wider bigger institution and have that sort of attitude.'

The school worked in many ways to address both the tensions in the relationships between boys and girls and to try and empower the girls and build their self-esteem. It pursued an ongoing policy of encouraging the girls to be assertive – the headteacher had organized an enthusiastic girls' football team and had initiated a mixed Scouts' group. The badminton club after school was also well attended and worked well, as both boys and girls competed on the same terms.

The head recognized the problems associated with this:

'The only trouble is are we doing them any favours? … You're in this terrible conflict, if we teach girls to behave in a certain way, and then they apply that at home, where do they fit in? If they're not accepted by their community who accepts them? If they're rejected by their community they're not part of mainstream society, so it's a real dilemma. But I think we've got to do what we feel is the right thing by the children and help them to cope in the wider world ... I'm sure the kids can cope, they understand that the situation is different and that in this area perhaps they have more freedom, perhaps they can express themselves more, perhaps they can push themselves more, but they realize that when they're at home it's different.'

Through talking to both boys and girls we had uncovered a variety of ways in which the children created their own identity, within the school environment as well as in their homes and religious communities. Ethnicity and gender recurred time and again as key issues in their identities. We had experienced at first hand how the school faced these tensions and conflicts and worked towards helping the children to be confident and happy in their own identity while at the same time respecting the diverse identities of people around them.

As the headteacher outlined:

'There is a conflict here, there is a clash because we're very hot on things like mixed gender, but then the community operates in a different way, but we've got to, from my point of view, we've got to try and produce kids who can operate in different spheres, who can quite happily operate in a mixed secondary school, or other spheres, but then cross the divide and come back into their community and be happy and work in their community structures as well.'

We have considered how the children spoke about the tensions within their communities of school and local area. However, a further issue the children face is that of moving on from the school environment, where at least they are able to recognize themselves as Asian among Asians. In the final part of this chapter I will look at how these Asian children identified themselves in the broader context of Britain and the wider world.

Moving on, an identity in the wider world

The school had worked hard and positively to address the tensions between the different ethnic groups in the school, and the headteacher describes very aptly how this is then reshaped by wider society, particularly when pupils go on to secondary school:

> 'The kids here are very, very happy and very secure. They are very secure in their identity and they draw themselves as black and very bold. When they go out from here there's a cultural blitz takes place and suddenly they're in parts of the city they've never been to before, under tremendous pressure because of where they come from in terms of the part of the city, it's got a low self-esteem in this part of the city, with prostitution and drugs and all the rest of it and also because of their background. So they meet racism for the first time maybe and they can become very introverted.'

The children were already aware of what it meant to be Asian in Britain and spoke of their own experiences of racism:

Q: Is there anything else wrong in the world do you think?

Y: People calling other people like, like us, like English people calling us Pakis and that, that should be changed.

Q: Do you experience some of that yourself?

Y: Sometimes, yes, like a gang will go up to people.

H: The NFs [*National Front*], they try to get us out of the city, they think this isn't our city, but do you know, India isn't our city either.

Q: So racism is the word you use, isn't it, to describe people like that, why do you think they're like that?

Y: It's because of our skin, like we're black and all that, dark brown and like you're a bit white and pink, that's why.

Q: Do you think there's anything you can do about it?

Y: Just be friends and all that.

H: Stay away from them.

Y: But if you stay away then you still meet them again and

they might think that, why are you staying away and they might concentrate on you even more.

From this we can see how Y and H:

- identify themselves as different, as black, or dark brown;
- find it difficult to locate themselves in any area because if this isn't their city and India isn't their home, where do they belong?
- show some fear and coping strategies to deal with those who inspire this fear.

The headteacher talks of the children coming out of their own 'miniworld'. From our interviews their sense of a wider identity and existence is very specific. They can enlarge their world geographically, not in terms of their identity as British but through those who share family connections, where their cousins and grandparents live:

J: I'd like to live in Kent, in Chatham, there's a place down there, I like it cos all my cousins are over there.

X: Guess where I'd like to live? I like to live in Birmingham, my cousin lives in Birmingham.

F: We've got about three cousins, some in Manchester and my grandma and my grandfather and my aunty, they gone, and my other aunty and my uncle and this little girl, their little baby, they've gone to Pakistan. My mum's going to go after two years, when two years comes, and my little brother and my little sister, when my mum comes then all in 1996, all of my family, all my cousins are going to go.

R: My dad's in Bangladesh, I'm going to go again with him when he comes back.

The children identify themselves as Asian but do not seem to think of themselves as British; instead their developing identity is focused on families, wherever they might be in the world, combined with the influences of ethnicity, religion and gender. Integration begins and ends with other Asians at school.

Where the wider world breaks in, the identity of these Asian children in Britain is frequently sabotaged. They are disadvantaged through their colour and cultural background, and, if girls, through their gender. This is forcibly brought home to them when they move on to secondary school. Once again the school we worked in was establishing links with other feeder schools, secondary schools and outside agencies to try and address the issues.

Conclusion

The identity of the boys and girls we talked to at this school was strongly established, with clear ethnic and gender differentiation. This may raise a number of issues educationally, as the school can be seen to address. The identity of these children in wider society perhaps raises a number of issues for us all to address, as a member of staff remarked:

'It's not to say that they cannot change, but they have to want to change, they've got to want to see that it's unfair ... it's like gender, if you're in a position of power you don't want to give the power up, so a female is oppressed and it's the same with race. White people are advantaged and they don't want to lose that advantage, you know, anyone who's coming up, if they get equal opportunities, they could be equal or better, but they can't cope with it, because they're a threat ... and a female from an ethnic minority is the most prejudiced group ... not only are they prejudiced because of their gender but also because of their culture, it is a waste ... I think that you've got to work at it all the time, it's no good doing it and then forgetting about it, I think this awareness-raising has to keep going on.'

7 Taking children's stories to other children

Clive Erricker

Introduction

This chapter describes how we decided to take the project one stage further towards realizing our aim of making its research available to schools and testing whether what we had already done was of some educational value. It is a case study, presenting the way in which previous research was introduced into a new school. It follows the process of children's responses to one child's account of the death of her grandmother (using V's story in Chapter 4, pages 47–8) with a Year 6 group.

Having interviewed children in five schools by this time, we now wished to use their words to invite children in other schools to talk about their experiences. We took a number of storied scripts to a school which was already asking children to discuss issues in regular year meetings and asked if they would be willing for us to come in and introduce their children to other children's stories. By reducing adult intervention in two respects – by providing a stimulus from another child, and by allowing children to talk to each other in larger groups – we intended to determine whether what we had already discovered was generally relevant to children's experience and could promote their development. Perhaps this idea could best be answered by the children themselves. When we subsequently put this question to one of the children she replied:

'I think it was valuable to ask us about our encounters with the deaths of our loved ones because it told other people that we all felt the same. We all felt upset and we could comfort each other.'

This response by one Year 6 child will later be contextualized within the responses of other children and those of the teachers concerned. At the outset, following a meeting with the teachers and headteacher, we collectively decided that the project's involvement would be incorporated into the programme of year assemblies. We would begin by taking a year assembly and interviewing children who wished to be interviewed afterwards. This programme was initiated in January 1996. We deliberately did not map out its development beyond the initial sessions in order to use the children's responses and involvement to determine how it should evolve. In this way we hoped to empower the children by emphasizing their ability to shape any subsequent planning; if it was in their agenda they would commit themselves to it, and if it didn't resonate with their experience we could revise our approach as a result. Subsequently, we were to realize the importance of this decision.

The Year 6 assembly

The first meeting with Year 6 included 60 children. We read out V's story as the stimulus. We were uncertain as to how 10- and 11-year-olds would react to the explanation of a 7-year-old child, but her age was not mentioned. As a strategy for response we gave the following instructions:

- think through what V said and whether you have experienced something similar in your lives;
- talk to each other if you wish and put up your hand if there is something you would like to say.

The tape recorder was passed to those who wished to speak. Each had a piece of paper and a pen on which to write down a response to V at the end of the session if they wished. If they were willing to talk further about what they had thought or written by being interviewed, they were asked to put a tick on their piece of paper.

Initially there was silence after the story. Concerned that

we had asked them to do something too difficult or too private in a meeting, I asked them if this was the case. A number of the children said 'No' in an emphatic fashion, but that they needed time to think about it. Conversation started, the atmosphere relaxed and the first hand, a boy's, was raised.

What followed, as the tape recorder was passed around the room, was a collection of stories expressing suppressed feelings of loss of different kinds, varying in intensity. By the end of the assembly ten children were crying, eight girls and two boys. Other children, both boys and girls, were comforting them. During the break some children wanted to talk further into the tape recorder. We then discussed with the teachers how best to follow up the situation. Since many of the children had explicitly stated during the assembly that they wanted to be interviewed and they expected to be interviewed after the break, as was our original intention, we had to decide if this was now the most appropriate action to take. The written responses give an indication of the intensity of the children's feelings and the pervasiveness of their felt need.

My uncle died from leukemia he was very good to me. Whenever we went to the farm he would let me go and milk the cows. My other uncle who owns the farm now won't let me milk the cows. But I still remember my uncle everytime I go up to the farm.

My important thing is when my nan got a disease she has lost her but I still see her she is very important to me I hope she does not die. She went into a home but she was to fit to stay there so my family looks after her but the thing is she doesn't know anything because she can't remember it so sometimes she forgets me. When she dies she will go up to heaven and I hope I will be able to see her when I die.

My Nan died when I was four and In my old house I saw my Nan on the celing she was burnt to I asked if I could go To the funnel but my mum said ide get to upset. When I saw my Nan on the celing she said be a good girl I will all wase be with you.

95

> Befor my nan died I used to go round every Sunday and see her I ran in and cuddle her

> My Nan was beried under a Tree well her ashes were anyway.

Of the 60 children present, 47 handed in written responses and some included pictures. Forty-five of those who responded mentioned the death of grandparents (30), uncles (three), animals (three), a sister, or the illness of a relative (four), which worried them. Five children mentioned more than one death. Some responded to V sympathetically, as follows:

> I know how she fills a few of my grand parents died went I was younger now I bleve there in heven now. (*Picture of two clocks and grandma and grandad with wings – like angels – on cloud.*)

> Dear V.
> I know how you feel I believe in heaven too. I expect she is having a wonderful time. My cat, dog and hamster have all died I hope they are happy. Lots of people have Diabetes in my family and one gran is very ill with it I write letters to her and I kind of send good thoughts and kind ones too. I expect your gran still loves you dearly.

> I think I know how you feel about your Grandma because a few months ago my Grandpa died and I still talk to his photo beside my bed and remeber him. Heaven is a wonderful place *I believe just paradise** for the best Grandpa ever. *He was always so happy all the time I loved you so much** who I love so dearly.
> [*words in italics crossed out]

Three children wanted to know what V's grandmother said to her when she 'rang up her brain':

> When your nan rings you up in your mind what does she say?
> My grandad died last year from a heart attack the first one was ok but the second killed him. (*Picture drawn in small box of figure lying on bed and something like a bolt of lightning coming down.*)

> When your nan rings you up in your brain what does she say

When your nan rings you in your brain does anyone else here you talking back

Three boys wrote about their parents' separation.

I rember when my mum and Dad split up I was very upset becaus my mum throw a shoe at my dad and take a chunk of skin out of dads face I still cry when my and mum met mum gets very upset so she always takes my out alote to stop he cry and get her mid of this. <u>Please read this.</u>

My mum and dad nearly split up. When my mum told me that she was moving into another house I was so upset. They are still married and will be moving back into the same house soon.

My mum and dad split up four years ago I feel angry partly with myself but mostly with my dad because he caused of the argument here is a pictur of what he done to my sister. (*Picture of a man standing behind a girl. The man is holding a knife labelled 'staber' and the girl is labelled 'sister' and is saying 'help'*)

The teachers' dilemma was created by the nature of the response. What had begun as an extension of the usual yearly meetings had turned into something the effect of which was significantly different. We had not been able to predict that effect. Although parents had been informed in a newsletter that this research was being carried out, subsequent reports home from upset children were likely to create worry and concern. Also, despite the children's wishes, we had to consider whether they would indeed benefit from further reflection on distressing memories and whether it might be better for them to be given more space to consider their request to talk further. Against this we genuinely wished to respond to the children and affirm their equal involvement. But did that place us, in the children's eyes, in the position of counsellors? This would present us with a responsibility which we would be unable to fulfil.

The teachers had the invidious responsibility of making the immediate decision as to whether to interview immediately or not, without recourse to consultation with the headteacher, who was out of school at the time. The decision was taken that we should not interview until we had had time to consult over the implications. We returned to the group to break the news.

We explained the difficulties that might result from interviewing them as planned and invited their responses. For the second time that morning I was told I was wrong. They insisted on their wish to be interviewed. We believed the authority did not lie with us. The teachers could not be sure of the outcome. The concluding decision was made that we would return the following week. Effectively we were buying time and a chance to reassess the situation. As researchers committed to empowering children and promoting their well-being, we felt we had not so far been successful and it might well be that the school did not feel this venture was worth pursuing any further.

Before the next session a meeting took place with the class teachers and headteacher. I sensed some uncertainty from the staff but the headteacher was happy for us to continue. I mention this because it does highlight the sensitive nature of the issues raised for schools in embarking on this kind of programme and the distinctiveness of the educational goals to which it relates. The implications with regard to resourcing, staff expertise and commitment and relations with children and parents are considerable, and involve an element of risk which many schools would consider neither realistic nor profitable. It raises further questions about the role of schools and the training of teachers as well as supplementary provision which, in the current climate, would have to be hard fought to gain acceptance as part of our educational duty.

The following week we agreed to take the assembly and talk further about interviewing. We also raised the question of whether the children felt it was acceptable to talk about this sort of issue and what other things they would like to discuss. The teachers were concerned about where this might lead, whether the children had been carried away by their emotions the first time and would feel differently on reflection.

The second assembly sparked a strong debate about what we were doing. Despite the majority of children who spoke wishing to affirm its value, two boys were adamant that it was unhelpful, arguing that it only upset people to go on about it and that it was better to talk about pleasant issues. One explained how, after the last assembly, he had cried in bed that night as a result of the way it affected him.

The children were asked again to write their comments on a sheet of paper and to tick a box if they wished to be interviewed. As before, a few children wanted to speak into the tape recorder after the meeting. We received 32 written comments, some of which were submitted by a pair or group of children. Sixteen wanted to be interviewed, two said they would not mind, three did not mention wanting to be interviewed but thought it was a good idea to talk about such things, and one wanted to talk about good things. Ten children did not want to be interviewed. The following examples express the forcefulness of feeling of some of the children.

> yes I want to be interviewed. My great grandad and grandma died in the war and I didn't get to see them. And my dog got put down because he broke his back. He was like my best friend. His name was Sandy. (*Then written upside down at the opposite end of the page*) I want to be interviewed but I don't want to be near anyone else. I would like to be alone.

I think it
would
be a
good idea
to talk
about
good
times

I wouldn't mind to be interviewed

YES I WOULD DEFINETLY LIKE FOR *SOMEONE** YOU TO
INTERVIEW ME ABOUT THINGS! ON MY OWN. OR <u>WITH
FRIENDS BUT</u> I HAVE QUITE ALOT OF ENEMYS AND I
WOULD NOT LIKE THEM TO HEAR
[*crossed out]

I think it would be nice if we could talk to people with the same
thoughts as us by recording messages on the tape recorder.

I would like to tell Clive about this
Its best to tell people to get it of our chest and have a cry because
my dad doesn't like my mum but I still love mum because I realy
haven't had lived with mum because I was 3 when mum moved.

talk about divorse
with children whos
parents are split
like me.

I would like to be interviewed

NO! (*Written large to fill the page*)
it was stupided of them to come in because it stated up memories
even thow you let your feelings out
And don't go on about it enymore
NO

Reviewing the responses with the headteacher helped us to
achieve a better understanding of some of them, particularly in
relation to one child, who had argued vehemently that talking
about these issues was not helpful, in the face of the comments
of most of the other children who insisted that such discussion
was valuable. His voice was prophetic in tone as though he were
addressing the children rather than just us. He was warning that
the result of this enterprise would be failure and disappoint-
ment. The reasons for this became clear when his own
experiences were recounted to us, during which he had been
counselled to the point of family therapy, when the hope of resolution to his own conflicts had foundered. This addressed one of

the main concerns that had emerged from the discussions with the children so far: their nervousness as to whether their parents would be consulted over what they had said or might say. Militating against this was a remark a parent had made to me at the school gates: she was pleased her daughter had taken part in the discussions and wished her to be interviewed in order to talk further about the death of her grandparent. This had been something she was reluctant to discuss at home but had valued discussing in the session in school.

The other significant issue to arise was expressed by one of the teachers at a subsequent meeting: that there was no way the teachers could cope with the demand of addressing the children's needs in terms of their time or their training. Unless this could be adequately resolved it was difficult to see how the issues that the project's involvement had raised could be addressed as an aspect of the school's provision.

The children's interviews

Over the following weeks we interviewed those Year 6 children who had put a tick on the paper. Some had asked to be interviewed alone or in pairs and others in small groups. The two major issues were the deaths of close relatives and the splitting up of families. Out of the discussion of these issues there arose an awareness of:

- The moral and spiritual maturity of children dealing with circumstances that they recognized as irresolvable.
- A recognition that children in these circumstances, more often than not, have no one they can talk to.
- A realization that if the children are given the sense that they can sort these issues out themselves, with support, that is exactly what they will do.
- A recognition that children wish to take responsibility for their own situation, they do not want adults to take it for them.
- An understanding that when we think of school provision we should think of the children as part of the provision, not as part of the problem.
- An understanding that if you treat children with respect and

integrity and communicate with them to resolve problems, that is
a sufficient aim. Ways forward will derive from that starting
point.

In summary, although there is no space in this chapter to
address the interviews in detail, the children who were significantly affected by the loss or conflict that they were
experiencing had found ways of coming to terms with it in
every case. What they felt a lack of was confirmation that
they were handling their situation correctly, and the awareness that they were not alone in dealing with these issues. In
the case of children with estranged parents they were fully
aware that their problems arose as a result of the parents no
longer liking one another, but realized that they could not
talk to them in order to put the situation right. They just
had to live with it. They were reluctant, in every case, to
blame their parents. Their realism was infused with compas-
sion for those they still loved. It was during the course of
the interviews that they came up with the strategy of forming
a self-help group where those who wished to talk through
their situation would meet regularly to do so, in the presence
of the headteacher. This is now in operation, a first step
forward.

We must bear in mind that the children in this school were
receiving support already from the implementation of a
school policy that encouraged active involvement in school
decision-making, concern for others and the development of
self-esteem and the shouldering of responsibility. Their home
backgrounds were also generally far more stable than those
of the children interviewed in the school described in Chapter
4. Nevertheless, in many respects, what was true of the children we interviewed in the one school was also true of those
in the other. In both situations the problem of conflict and
loss was pervasive, the children experienced a need to
address it and parents and teachers, for different reasons,
were often not seen as the appropriate adults to approach.
By pursuing the research in a second school, we became

aware that it required an outside agency to identify their individual needs and help them to create an appropriate environment in which they could be expressed, with the assistance of the staff.

8 Children and parental separation

Clive Erricker

This chapter follows on from the work reported in Chapter 7. In response to the story about the loss of V's grandmother we received numerous accounts of the effect of bereavement from other children, but we also received accounts of the sense of loss experienced by children whose parents had split up or in whom they felt unable to confide. This mirrored the findings we had previously received at the beginning of our research. We followed these up with interviews in this school in order to explore further the effect of this situation upon the child and the provision that might be required. We bore in mind that the catchment area was significantly different and that this might well affect the outcome in terms of provision and the possibilities relating to home–school liaison.

It is significant that the children in this school raised the issue of parental separation as being of concern in a number of their lives, echoing what we had discovered in conversation with children earlier in our research, reflecting a larger social debate referred to frequently in the media and evidencing a current focus of political concern. It is significant that, though this debate figures strongly in our concern for children's and society's welfare, there is little said about the role of schools and education generally in addressing the issues it raises. Perhaps it is the case that, by focusing so hard on the curriculum, we have actually lost sight of the larger and more integral role that schools have to play in the personal and social development of children. As a result, the most significant aspect of this – the relationships established between teachers, parents and welfare agencies – has been ignored at the same time as parental choice has been affirmed. On the surface this is a curious irony but on closer inspection it presents itself as a more worrying phenomenon. It suggests that the notion of parental choice is circumscribed by a limitation to curriculum and academic fulfilment. It is a way of fencing off schooling from a broader and more holistic notion of education that is founded on relationships rather than things. We want to address the contemporary problem of an increasing divorce rate but do not think it is necessary to talk to or listen to children in order to do so. Thus it is conceived as an adult problem but it is, in fact, a people problem and an educational one, at root. I say this because I have been persuaded to this view by the children we have spoken to and the research we have undertaken.

In an article in the *Guardian* entitled 'Should I stay or should I go' (27 March 1996) it was suggested that unhappy parents should stick together for the sake of the children. Would that it were that simple. The most constructive statement was made by Peter Wilson, the director of Young Minds:

> Seeing parents filled with hatred and out of control, and especially seeing one parent being hurt, can be very frightening and damaging. But if parents can show children that there can be strong disagreements and life can still carry on, that could be useful. What is very important is that children are not ignored, and treated as if they don't exist, or as if nothing has happened.

The last statement made by Wilson is the most important one. Yes, outcomes are important, but processes are even more so. Whatever the outcome, in terms of separation or not, the children's understanding of what has happened and why will be the legacy by which they are limited or liberated in later life.

Our first question, consistent with the project's overall approach, concerned what exactly was the child's perception of his or her experience and what effect it had upon his or her outlook and needs. The following account relates to the responses of six children, but focuses on an interview with two boys who had most assertively asked to be interviewed about their experience, and wished to be interviewed together. To ensure the depth of analysis required this report mainly narrates the situation described by one of these children. The initial stimulus for the interview, as with the others, was the written responses the children had offered at the end of the assembly.

Analysis of the children's conversations identified the importance of the following issues:

- the effect of the situation upon the child
- the reasons for the situation occurring
- the outcome the child envisages
- the response of the school to the situation investigated.

These have not been delineated in a systematic order but can be identified in the context of the ensuing commentary.

The two boys, L and G, describe a situation in which their parents split up some time ago, but the event continues to have a significant effect on their lives, since it has an underlying influence on their outlook, the way in which they understand themselves in relation to their peers and the way in which they think their peers perceive them.

It is important to mention, at the outset, that all the children involved wished to affirm their support for and love of their parents, and they continually made this clear throughout the interviews; however, this did not prevent them from having a distinct and objective view of the situation. In fact what was so impressive was the realism with which they were able to evaluate their circumstances, combining understanding and sympathy with rational judgement.

G spoke of the problems he faces living with his dad and being separated from his mum:

> It's really hard for me, my mum split up with my dad and I don't know what it's really like to have a mum cos I wasn't old enough to know when they split up and I'd just like to go and see her more often cos all I hear of her are like phone calls or I go and see her about once a year.

The distress at not seeing his mother is compounded by his dad's attitude to the situation:

> Like me and my dad, if like, I'm frightened to say if I could go and see my mum and he's saying no, you've got to stay here. Like the other day Dad was in the room and I was saying 'Why can't I go and stay with Mum?' and he just came over and hit me, I can never mention Mum when he's in a mood.

In G's account what was to become a familiar pattern emerges. First, there are the unanswered questions as to why his parents split up and why he cannot see his mother more often. To some degree he knows the answers, since he is aware that his parents did not get on and that his father does not like his mother. Beyond this, however, a situation has emerged in which G seeks to retrieve the past while his father strives to forget it. G's questions and his desire to see his mother more often compound his father's guilt and difficulty in creating a new life for himself. His inability to address G's needs, however, simply exacerbates the situation. If G cannot talk to his father in order to understand the past, address the present and resolve the future, who can he talk to? The emotional tension created expresses itself in his father's violent response. Where no rational solution can be envisaged, the inner rage and confusion erupts in irrational violence.

G's difficulties are compounded by his concern for his mother in her estranged situation. The parents split up when he was 3 and his subsequent contact with her which he mentions above has been infrequent.

In the intervening time her history has separated from his and G's perception of it pictures her as in need of support. The sketchiness of his familiarity with her situation also leaves him anxious and yet unable to involve himself or do anything to help.

> That's another thing about my mum as well, another reason why she's distressed, she found another man, she had

another baby, but she couldn't cope, where she had no money and everything, that baby had to go into foster care, and I only saw him once, he's my only like stepbrother.

As the picture unfolds, we see G trying to hold together a situation that is at the mercy of the forces of emotional embitterment and accumulated stress. Unlike G, his two sisters have no wish to see their mother. He has no knowledge of the whereabouts of his stepbrother and he sometimes fears he will lose touch with his mother completely.

She just lives in——, but when we don't hear from her we think maybe she doesn't live there any more, so we don't know where to go if we want to see her.

Listening to G brought to my mind images and stories that acquired greater significance in the light of his narrative. At an early age he embodies what the artist Rouault had depicted in his painting 'The Hard Business of Living'. G's circumstance could also be seen as a poignant contemporary expression of the complex message of the Adam and Eve story of the Fall, in that he seeks to accomplish the reconciliation required within a situation of which he is the inheritor and, as a result, a necessary though not a willing participant. The notion of inheritance is particularly significant in the sense of the negative internal energy that has to be channelled and dissipated. At the beginning of the interview both G and L were asked to introduce themselves. In doing so G, like many other children, mentioned something which is particularly important to him.

Hi, I'm G and I've learnt to play football.

Later, an unexpected significance is attached to this.

L explains how the sense of exclusion resulting from being kept in the dark about things compounds the frustration he feels, which then results in violent outbursts. Both boys then relate the way in which playing football provides a therapeutic release.

L: A lot of things are kept secret aren't they?

G: Yeh ...

L: Yeh, it happens all the time. My mum, cos like sometimes I get like my dad and I get really angry and
sometimes I hit people too, like my sisters, and I know
and I don't do that any more, I take it out on like sports
and stuff.

Q: Does sport help?

L: Yeh, a lot.

G: Yeh, a lot.

L: You really think that, you're aiming at something, really
push it to the limit.

G: It's like kicking a football, you really take it, you really
kick it really hard, like get your stress out of you and
that and just enjoy yourself where you are.

L: It just builds up during the week and Saturdays and
Sundays you just really go for it.

The boys recognize the value of football as a displacement
activity, but it goes further than that. It provides a sense of
achievement that they cannot get elsewhere and reorients their
world by allowing them to live in the present, regardless of the
surrounding complications in their lives which they cannot
resolve. But, most important, they become normal, carefree
children, not defined by their anomalous social situation and
the stigma attached to it. To use G's phrase, when speaking of
the value of going away on a school holiday with his friends,
it 'refreshes our memories'.

Talking about the situation has a similar effect:

G: Talking's the best way to get it off your mind a lot, cos
well you get the chance to talk about things, cos this is
the first time we've actually got to just discuss it with
somebody. But if it was like a group or a class of children, about ten people, I couldn't say anything then cos
I'd be scared cos I would think people might take the
mickey out of me.

109

L: If there's someone in your class who's in the same situation, like me and G, it's good to talk to each other and comfort each other.

That's what I was thinking about when you first came in and all the girls were crying. I thought like you've really helped them, like it was talking about what really happened to them.

This point about addressing children's actual experiences is at the heart of the issue. L's comment implicitly identifies what both school and home do not address, for differing reasons. As a result the children build up a network among friends who have undergone similar experiences and, as a result, can offer understanding. L and G explain:

G: But one time I got really, I got so sad about it. But somebody asked me and I just, I told three of my friends, B, N and D, what had happened, they understood.

L: I talked to N about what had happened to me, he was another person I thought I could talk to because he's, his mum and dad were on the verge of splitting up and he felt what I felt then and he, he keeps it a secret.

This initiative of the children themselves was the clue as to how to develop provision. Talking with friends was not quite enough but it gave them ideas.

G: The thing is I like talking about it with an adult.

G's comment fired their imagination and, with the confidence they had gained from the discussion, led them to approach the headteacher and ask her to set up a group to discuss these issues. As a result, the self-help group mentioned in Chapter 7 was formed. It was called 'The Meeting'. As a commentary on progress so far, at the time of writing, it is probably best to record it in the headteacher's own words in her correspondence with me.

I have enclosed a section from my Headteacher's report to the governors in which I had reported on the work you had been doing in school. The response was very positive and they are supportive of initiatives of this sort. Two governors have children in year 6 – one of whom is happy to continue discussions and another who enjoyed his 'interaction' with you but does not wish it to go any further. Both governors however felt very comfortable with the work you had done and were very supportive.

As a result of your work a group of children have chosen to continue meeting as an extra to 'The Meeting' (at the first occasion of which 40 children attended).

I keep a special box in my room in which they can write down problems they are experiencing (confidentially if they choose). Those problems are the basis for discussions. A group of three pupils chair and manage these meetings (I just oversee them and offer my support *only* when asked)

They have all negotiated and agreed 'ground rules'. These meetings will continue this term.

However, she also commented:

I already work approximately 70 hours a week (a lot of these at school) and given the current curriculum content and government legal requirements on which we are inspected I feel 'torn'. It seems that school is having to (and being expected to) take on more and more responsibility without adequate time, support and resources. We need the resources to employ a counsellor who can work with individuals and groups outside the classroom (the sort of role you came in and took on). We *need* this *need* to be recognised and addressed. It needs to be a teacher who has been trained to counsel who understands the 'whole' child. Where do we start??

Barbara Ward comments:

During the school years about 20 per cent of all children will at some time experience being identified as having special educational needs ... These difficulties can result in loss of status, self esteem, friends, participation in activities, achievements, and sometimes loss of family, the degree of loss will depend on the child's perception and the reaction of those around them.

(Ward *et al.*, 1995, p. 11)

Ward takes her percentage figure from the DFE (1994). In relation to our findings on the project's research, and especially in terms of the response of the children in this one, fairly representative school, a further provision is required. This should not be identified as special needs but neither is it straightforward curriculum provision. The problem is the identification of what we might call these 'experiential needs'. Why should this be so? We suggest that the problem arises because of the perception that events such as those recorded above are only recognized when they are designated under the title of special needs. In other words, they are only understood to have happened to a child once an effect on their learning is identified. On the contrary, from the children's point of view, their intention in dealing with such events is to keep them to themselves until such time as the effect of these events impinges on their learning or behaviour in school. At this point it is more often the teacher rather than the child who determines that they require special needs provision. For those children who are not identified in this way, the legacy of events still has its impact. But, because it is not revealed in their classroom performance, it remains unaddressed. Nevertheless, once given the opportunity to bring it to the surface children readily take it, since parents and friends, their other outlets to communicate their concerns, tend to be inappropriate or insufficient mediators for this information. This points to the need for schools to readdress their educational priorities and the breadth of their provision if they are willing to understand their role in a manner which takes account of the needs of the whole child.

With regard to Ward's final comment, the project's research emphatically endorses its importance. However, the children's perceptions and reactions of those around them are heavily influenced by the variant particulars of the home situation and the vision of education identified in the school's policy statement and government priorities for education. Beyond this, children can only rely on the character and responsiveness of individual teachers and headteachers.

References

Ward, B. and Associates (1995) *Good Grief: Exploring Feelings, Loss and Death with Under Elevens*. London, Jessica Kingsley.
Wilson, P. (1996) Should I stay or should I go. *Guardian*, 27 March.

9 Religious identity and children's worldviews

Mandy Fletcher and Cathy Ota

Introduction

This chapter considers children nurtured in a distinctive religious context. Using data from two different types of community we wish to explore the way in which the nurture of a child into a particular religious identity can be seen to significantly affect the child's worldview – that is, their understanding of themselves, their experiences and the way they relate to the world and other people around them.

The children featured in this chapter come from two very different types of 'nurture bases'. Mandy's research looks at the beliefs and worldviews of New Age children in Somerset and Devon, while Cathy's focuses on two boys and two girls who were interviewed at an evangelical Christian school in south-east England.

Mandy's research

In recent years in Britain the New Age has reached sufficient size and coherence to be recognized as a discernible movement. It is comprised of seemingly disparate groups which adopt both ancient and modern beliefs and philosophies; this creates an eclectic, holistic outlook on life which characterizes New Age beliefs and concerns. The New Age approach to life centres around the healing of body and mind, reincarnation, Divine Energy, or God, a sense of a higher self and complementary medicines. Although various groups may accentuate different elements, there is a general focus on a deep knowledge of the self and God, in whatever way it may be expressed.

Making contact with New Age groups

In the summer of 1995 several weeks were spent in Somerset and Devon identifying families with children who could be interviewed for this study. As there are no New Age schools, I went to areas which are well known for New Age activity, the first objective in each location being to find a likely New Age contact centre. In this way I was able to get names of parents with suitable children.

The interviews

Seventeen children were interviewed in all: eight boys and nine girls. As it was the summer holidays all the children were interviewed in their own homes, usually in the presence of their mothers.

As a way of getting them started and providing an open framework to work in, each child was asked to draw a picture of the most important or special thing to them in life; this was discussed and the interview continued, following whatever topics the child raised. I hoped this would enable them to express their own concepts and ideas and the things that were personally significant to them. After the main interview several artefacts which have strong New Age connections were shown. The children were asked to explain as much as they knew about each item – in some cases this produced valuable information which complemented and extended the data from the initial interview.

Key themes

During the interviews I was looking for things that the children mentioned which might not be discussed by children from different backgrounds. Along with their families, other themes that appeared prominently were healing and crystals, which introduced their understanding of the relationship between themselves and the natural world.

Several children drew pictures of the world or nature and

eight of the children discussed it during the interview. For all of them there was an interconnectedness between being alive, living in nature and the planet itself; what is interesting is that none of these themes appeared in isolation, as C illustrates:

C: I like the world because if it wasn't for the world I wouldn't be here ... I love it because all my family live on it and I love them so I just love it really ... all the animals that live on it and I like to swim in the sea and I like climbing trees and playing on the fields and stuff like that ... it makes me feel nice and stuff. ... My life is very special, I wouldn't want to die now, not when I'm young, and I don't want to grow up either. I just like being little, but sometimes it's quite a drag.

S, aged 12, is another example from several children who began by voicing a concern about this planet, and moved directly on to the importance of nature and their love for it, and then on to the nature of life, living and death. Her perception of life seemed on a global rather than local scale:

S: I think the most important thing in life is 'life' and um because I was thinking of it in an overall view. The most important thing in anything is life, and how it is lived by different people because that is what they think about most, because if you weren't here you wouldn't be alive.

Q: So what's important about life?

S: Well everything is around life and everything is about life, really like the simplest thing is alive ... it's like when something is dead it isn't here any more and so when you're alive that's the most important thing.

Q: What do you mean by the simplest thing?

S: Well, even something like a dandelion ... or a beetle ... it has a life and it lives its life and it has something to do doesn't it? ... So that's the most important thing, keeping alive.

Q: Do you mean keeping alive or living your life?

S: I think living your life, it's doing what you do in life, like you do everything to keep yourself happy, to keep yourself alive, I don't know it's quite complicated.

These children have a vision of life as being more sacred than most children of their age would understand and that vision of life includes all other species. They see themselves as an intrinsic part of the natural world. Their classification is entirely inclusivist in that they do not seek to make divisions between the value of different life forms or the value of different human belief systems. The significant judgement is made on the basis of life being seen to be valued in its different manifestations.

Crystals and healing were the focus of further conversations throughout the interviews; they were also the areas of conversation which created the most excitement in the children. From their comments it seems that the children are in the process of developing new ideas and folklore around this area, as is illustrated in the following extracts.

Crystals

Every child interviewed in Somerset mentioned crystals.They were often discussed in connection with healing, as some of these comments illustrate:

R: They're purple ... it's a stone that shines and you can do healing with it ... if you are sick or something it can help it away.

J: I don't really know all the names but I think it's an amethyst ... it's got some healing power.

Q: Do you ever use them for that?

J: Yeh, sometimes.

R: That one is another crystal, it's rose quartz ... that one is for the heart isn't it Mum? Yes, for headaches too and the heart.

This demonstrates the growing folklore around the subject of crystals and the ever-increasing list of the properties they possess: healing, containing power, relating and acting upon the chakras (energy centres through the body), warding off bad spirits and bad dreams, used as birthstones, symbolizing purity, helping you sleep, removing headaches, removing pain, ornamental, representing the earth and love, and being used in ceremonies.

C is just one of the children who discussed crystals at some length with me:

> C: Well I like the colours and the shapes, and some of them I feel like I've got a strong feeling for ... it may be the power of it or something like that ... it's powerful power ... it's like nature, it's growing ... I think the power of nature makes the power of the crystal but it's a different kind of power ... There's a type of crystal for the chakra set and I've got a set and I've been looking out about what they say for the seven chakras. I think some of them are quite powerful.

Evident in the above conversation is the child's belief that power in the sense of positive energy can be communicated through a particular object with certain physical attributes. The physical attributes of clean, sharp lines, translucent appearance, clear colour and strength can be seen as metaphors for purity, clarity of vision and immortality. We are not saying that the child is articulating this directly, but that there is a subliminal message in the child's conversation, perhaps inculcated through parental influence, that points in this direction.

It is fascinating to note that these children will communicate these ideas, which are far removed from the accepted notions of the majority of their peers outside their community and might well be ridiculed by those peers. In a larger context within which their understanding would not only seem implausible but bizarre, because of the connections they make between the physical and the metaphysical, we might expect them to conform to more conventional views. It appears to be the case that the relative balance between parental nurture and schooling has had a significant influence on their thinking.

Nearly all of the children interviewed owned a crystal, some had many, and they were valued highly as prized possessions. Some children discussed other aspects of healing.

Healing

J, aged 10, tried to explain what healing was:

> J: I have to go to healing on Tuesdays and Fridays ... healing's a bit like Reiki, or Reiki's like healing ... Reiki is where you heal different parts of your body in a special way, it's like medicine coming out of your hands ... I did some for Mum, I did some for D once and Mummy's done some for me. You just put your hands on the place and ... what happens is that you think about healing the person you're healing and it happens.
>
> Q: Just like that?
>
> J: No, sometimes it takes a long way to get through. Like tubes it runs through. Sometimes it gets stuck and it hurts a bit and there might be a bit of blocking, which happened to me once when I lay on the couch. And it hurts in some places and not in others, it goes quite smoothly.

For J, the issue of healing is not a matter of simply curing a physical ailment by means of conventional medical intervention. Instead it is a holistic process whereby a particular problem is dealt with by means of a transference of energy from the healer to the healed. This accords with the overall view that healing is not a piecemeal process of putting something right but re-balancing the overall well-being of the organism. Again we are not suggesting that J has thought the matter through this far, but his thinking is conversant with this paradigm.

D, aged 6, is J's brother and he too gives healing on a regular basis, although in some ways aspects of his opinions can be seen to be quite different to his brother's:

D: When you give it to someone else it feels warm on them, you actually giving them healing energy from the cosmos.

Q: What's the cosmos?

D: It's kind of like Jesus and it gives you healing energy. You're giving them healing energy, more energy, you put your hands on anywhere they've hurt themselves or you want it. You don't actually have your hands on your knees, you put them near to the knees and it goes up the knees.

Q: And when you touch them does your body feel warm or is it their body that feels warm?

D: It's their body. I felt it myself and it is different from people touching you normally. It also feels nice, that's what I can say.

D makes use of 'Jesus' as a concept to express the cosmos and its energy. Earlier in the interview he also spoke about God:

D: Um, excuse me, you know R didn't know what God was, it's a huge clump of energy, that's all. Just a big clump of energy like a man and he's wearing a white cloak. He is, I've seen it in a story.

This highlights the way in which both home and school play a role in the nurturing of children's belief structures and worldviews. D and J go to the local state school and their mother mentioned how they were concerned about what was taught by way of religious education and that they were not happy with what they saw as indoctrination, which appeared to confuse the boys. Certainly both the boys talked about their experiences of healing and God's energy and they also made use of Christian Bible stories and Jesus.

What D had done was to construct a synthesis of what he had learned at home and at school. (In a similar way the children featured in Chapter 5 put together religious and scientific concepts.) D had linked his ideas of energy and the cosmos with Christian religious concepts and representations of God and created his own picture. There is no confusion evident in what D says, just a composite construction. It may of course not be what D's parents would prefer, and this underlines the difficulty in working between what schools deliver as appropriate religious education and what parents of particular persuasions might wish their children to receive.

In contrast, the mother had been trained through the National Federation of Spiritual Healers and in Reiki, which is Japanese in origin and is concerned with restoring life energy. One can recognize the influence of the mother's training in what the boys discuss. It is perhaps neither possible nor helpful to identify what sort of healing the boys are using. Instead it might be argued that they are employing a third kind of healing, slightly removed from any received dogma, emerging from the boys' nurturing influences, together with their own interpretations and experiences.

Further examples of the connection between experience and belief

Other children also demonstrated the way in which direct experiences affected belief. For example, S mentioned that she used incense and Tibetan bells (Buddhist in origin) to clear the room of bad energy. She explained how she used a dream catcher (North American Indian in origin) to catch her bad dreams, although it had not worked recently because the family had recently moved and she had hung it too far from her bed.

Another child, T, said he kept a dark crystal to stop himself having bad dreams and he also used a bunch of herbs known as smudge (used by North American Indians), which is lit to keep the bad spirits away. For T, both the crystal and the smudge are used for protection.

New Age beliefs and worldviews

All the reports from the children are highly experiential and they treat the metaphysical as quite normal. This in turn fosters an acceptance of spirituality. The children from this nurturing background appear to be eclectic and incorporate the metaphysical into their everyday lives. By actively putting into use things like crystals, incense and dream catchers they are able to recognize and combat their fears – it may be argued that this use of artefacts helps to psychologically enable the child. Although within the New Age there is no doctrinal authority there is a strong experiential element and this has been shown to be prominent in the children to whom I spoke.

The children demonstrated various concepts and beliefs associated with the New Age. This may also be seen to contribute to the way the children showed an extensive amount of affective thinking and emotional intelligence in their discussions about their experiences and relationships with objects and the world.

We will explore the implications this has for education after looking at Cathy's research with children nurtured in a particular Christian belief.

Cathy's research

Background to the study

I made contact with the headteacher of the school in 1995 after a discussion with a teacher in the local area. The headteacher was very welcoming and it was decided that I would work with Year 6. Although I interviewed the whole class in groups of six, I will concentrate here on two longer interviews I conducted afterwards. The first interview was with two girls, L and U, and the second with two boys, T and S. What I soon discovered was that the four children had very different levels of nurturing in terms of Christian belief. The girls described themselves as very committed to God and much of the interview focused on illustrating this with descriptions of aspects of their lives and relationships. The boys had a more questioning approach to their belief in God and its implications, and this can be seen to shape their worldviews quite differently from the girls.

Nurturing a religious identity – the fundamental role of the family

Several key themes emerged from the interviews which illustrate the children's perception of their religious identity and the effect of this nurture on their outlooks. They all emphasized commitment, belonging and belief as fundamental to being a Christian and of great importance to them personally. They drew on examples from their family and referred to authority figures to demonstrate this. L highlights this in her discussion:

> L: I can't really help thinking about it [being a Christian] cos of my mum ... whenever my brother or my sister are naughty she starts saying things like 'if you were a proper Christian you wouldn't have done that' and things like that, I don't really get to hear the end of it.
>
> Q: So your mum talks a lot about what being a Christian is like, does your dad?
>
> L: Not really, cos my dad was Catholic but he's not really that committed.
>
> Q: So you learn more from your mum?
>
> L: Yeh, cos whenever me, my brother or my sister are ill and can't go to church, then it's my dad who stays behind, he's not that bothered about not going ... he does go sometimes but he says it's boring and he just walks out ... I think my mum does get a bit, 'well I do wish you would be a bit better Christian', I think that I wish he was a better Christian because my mum has said that I can get baptized when my dad agrees to it and my dad says that I've got to be the most perfect Christian ever before I can be baptized and he's been baptized himself and he's not a Christian!

Some immediate observations can be drawn from L's discussion about her family:

- the fundamental role of the family in identifying and promoting certain values;
- the authority L recognizes in her mother because she is the one

123

who lives out these values of commitment, belonging and belief, whereas her father does not;

- the values identified and promoted as those required to be a good Christian are commitment and belief – L expresses in no uncertain terms her own strong sense of commitment and belief;
- L's personal sense of belonging and identity in being a Christian and the security it provides for her.

At other times during the interview L referred again to the key role of family in nurturing a Christian religious way of living which extended from everyday matters to addressing fundamental existential issues, such as death:

> L: When I was on holiday one time I was getting quite a bit worried about what it might be like when I died cos somebody had told me about a plane crash … and I asked my mum what it would be like if we died and … I was trying this new ice-cream, orange sorbet, that I'd never had before … and she said 'Well I think it'll be like trying a new ice-cream, you know you'll like it but you're not sure what it's gonna taste like' … and that's what I've thought ever since really cos we know that it's gonna be lovely there … I believe that when you die your soul goes to heaven and it's put into a new body.

L subsequently continued.

> L: Well, my gran, her husband died … and I remember thinking when he died … I wasn't sure where he'd go cos we believe that if you're a Christian you go to heaven and if you're not you go down to hell and if he wasn't a Christian for most of his life, and when he became ill with cancer Gran was desperately trying to get him to become a Christian and he started coming along to church, he sort of went for about two weeks and then he became too ill to go so he couldn't cos he was in hospital. So Gran was never really sure whether or not he had become a Christian, she was just talking to him and he couldn't really answer. And then he died, then after a while Granny started saying that he was a

Christian. I think it was more to do with that she was thinking 'I don't want to think that he's not in heaven, I just want to get the memory away from me'.

Q: So is that what you believe as well, you say that's what your family believes but do you think that as well?

L: Yeh.

Q: And is that true of the church and the school as well?

L: Well, it's definitely true of the church, I'm not really sure about the school, I think that most people who are Christians think that.

Just as the beliefs of the New Age children helped them to confront their fears, L's belief, through the enabling influence of her family, helps her to consider something she finds quite scary – the thought of dying. On the other hand, its exclusivist nature presents problems when it is a close family member who is excluded, in this case her grandfather who has died and she is not sure if he was a Christian and so might not be in heaven. L shows a remarkable understanding of her grandmother's state of mind, such that she could not encompass the idea of her grandfather not being included in the comfortable vision of an afterlife.

T and S employ their own ideas and Christian beliefs to address existential issues, making use of concepts related to God and life after death.

Q: Is there anything you worry about at all that you might pray about?

T: Um, death really, what's gonna happen to you when you die.

S: Yeh, but I mean you're gonna die someday aren't you?

T: Yeh, but I reckon when you die, you have another life, like some other thing.

Q: Like reincarnation?

T: Yeh.

S: I don't know about reincarnation though, well like the population's growing every day, like say five people die, then ten people are born.

125

Q: So where do you think they go, S?

S: Heaven.

Q: And what do you think heaven might be like?

S: Well people say it's got streets of gold but you never know until you get there and then it's too late to come back and tell everyone ... there was this bloke at church, he said he'd been to heaven and back, he said he'd died and come back.

Q: And do you believe him?

S: He could have done I suppose, but nobody knows really.

Q: Do you think everyone goes to heaven?

S: Well, I don't know really, maybe.

T: I think maybe everyone would go to heaven actually, even if you didn't believe in God because it's –

S: Well, no!

T: Well what my mum says is that um, well like soldiers of war who didn't believe in God were dying in their beds, they say 'I believe in God' and then when they die they go to heaven.

Q: But if you didn't believe in God you wouldn't?

T: Well I don't know ...

S: Maybe you would.

T: You don't know do you? You don't know until you get there and then it's too late to come back

Q: Why do you believe in God?

S: Cos everybody else tells you to, they say like when you die you want to go to heaven and you don't really want to go to somewhere horrible and if you don't believe in God that he's true then you will go there.

Q: So if you didn't believe in God you'd go somewhere horrible?

S: You don't really know that but you don't really want to like take the chance either.

T: I reckon there is such a thing as a heaven, but someone else runs it maybe.

Q: Not God you mean?

T: Well God might or Jesus might.

Q: How does Jesus and God fit together?

S: I don't know that, they say they're one, but I don't really know that, nobody knows that.

T: People say that when they die they're gonna live again, that's what the Hindus think isn't it?

The boys' approach and use of a religious identity is very different from that of the girls I interviewed:

- Rather than exclusivist it is more open and flexible, acknowledging and weighing up a much wider vision which may or may not be incorporated into their personal worldview.
- T's mum, like L's, has an important role in nurturing her child's approach to life, although in T's case it does not automatically exclude people with other beliefs, but instead tries to take them into account.
- There is a sense of an ongoing search for meaning and discovery about God, rather than a defined, rigid framework within which L seems to work.

The nurturing of the families of these children empowers them to feel secure and confident in who they are, enabling them to establish a coherent worldview which helps them to deal with life and relationships. The family can certainly be defined as the most significant influence; however, it is perhaps worth noting how, to a lesser degree, both the church community and school also contributed to their sense of Christian identity.

T and S have already alluded to the role of the church in exploring the issue of death. L and U refer more explicitly to the way the church community helps to create a strong Christian identity for them, but not without tensions:

L: I quite like coming to this school but sometimes I wish I didn't go here because at my church where I go they're always talking about like 'try and tell everybody at school about becoming Christian' and I keep thinking, but practically everyone in my school is a Christian, so what can I do about it?

127

Q: They tell you that at church?

L: Yeh, they just say try and get as many of your friends to become Christians as you can and I sort of think, all my friends are Christian, they all go to church regularly.

There is a sense in which the girls adopt a different 'Christian' identity from the boys. Although the boys employ the concepts and utilize their Christian nurture in their outlooks and attitudes, the girls seemed to reveal a deeper personal, experiential side to their belief and faith. Later in the interview both L and U discussed the personal relationship they felt they had with God:

U: (*on death*) I don't really think about it much but when I do and if I get worried I just think it doesn't matter cos God's gonna take charge of it.

Q: Hmm, is it a nice feeling to think of God being there?

L: Yeh ...

U: In charge.

Q: And do you think that if God's always there and in charge, do you think that God can see what you're doing?

L: Yeh ... it says in the Bible that God knows what's gonna happen before it happens and I really believe that.

Q: Is that a nice feeling knowing that?

L: I don't know cos when I go wrong in my prayers or something, like if I'm saying something and I describe it wrong or something.

U: Or like if it doesn't make sense.

L: Yeh, or if I change my mind or something, I don't really like knowing that God knew that I'd made a mess of it.

Q: Do you pray on your own at all?

U: I sometimes pray in bed but I don't do it every night, I usually just pray when I need to.

Q: Do you pray on your own at all, L?

L: Yeh, with my gran I don't really say no cos she likes us to pray when we go to sleep and we say things like 'dear Lord, thank you for today, thank you for mummy and daddy, please keep them healthy, thank you for my brothers and sisters', we say things like that and I don't really think that's the right type of prayer.

U: Yeh, that's like you're just saying oh I'm brilliant cos I'm praying, I don't need to do anything else.

Q: So what would be a good sort of prayer?

U: Something straight from the heart.

L: Yeh, anything that's straight from the heart and it's not just thought out in your brain and let out from your mouth.

U: If it's the type of thing you say everyday it doesn't have any feeling in it.

From these transcripts of our interviews with L and U we can see how, although they refer to authority such as the grandmother or the Bible, they also incorporate their own interpretation and understanding of what God is like and what prayer should be.

We have seen how both the boys and girls show varying degrees of personal reflection on their own interpretation of themselves and the world, and in each instance it is the family background which is fundamental in shaping the type of nurture and values which the child expresses. This may be distinguished as inclining to an inclusivist or exclusivist understanding in different cases, but it is the tension between the two that creates the greatest concern.

The girls displayed many signs of viewing the world in an exclusivist way, where everything is divided into 'us' and 'them' – the 'us' being Christians. This makes the girls feel secure and defines a clear sense of identity for them; however, in a different context such an approach may in fact be disabling for the child concerned.

The boys also demonstrated an awareness of different people in the world, but this was expressed in a more inclusivist way, perceiving themselves as being just as different as everyone else:

Q: Do you pray a lot in school?

T: We pray every day ... sometimes you're thinking if someone walked through the door and they didn't know anything about Jesus, they'd think we were a load of nutters or something.

Nurturing children – some general comments and educational implications

There is much we could comment on here, and perhaps what is interesting is that although the children have very different types of nurture, when viewed together they highlight several points for consideration:

- Nurture, to varying degrees, affects the child's worldview in terms of characteristics, concepts, attitudes and understanding of themselves.
- The nurture provided is often valuable for the child in helping them to develop a strong sense of identity and belonging, which is important to them.
- It helps them to understand and maintain relationships within their family.
- It helps them to confront and deal with their fears and further existential issues.
- Although this nurturing may be seen in one context as enabling for the child it may or may not present problems as different children in different communities try to engage with each other and communicate as they mature into adulthood.

Educationally speaking, we believe there are certain issues which need to be carefully considered by educationalists and schools alike. We need to be aware that within the same religious tradition different attitudes may exist, fostered by different parents and groups, that shape children's understanding in alternative ways. This is especially the case in relation to others who do not share similar beliefs in themselves, their family or their community. The notions of exclusivism and inclusivism are important in this respect. We must appreciate that certain exclusivist notions of identity may be enabling in a particular context with respect to security, confirmation of faith, or the bonding of a group (family or community), but may well result in difficulty when those in the group seek to communicate and understand themselves and others in a wider context. It is also important to recognize the value that metaphysical and imaginative thinking of a religious kind can have for children in an emotional sense: allaying fears and creating security. This is often communicated through the use of symbols and ritual actions. Religious nurture appears to be a two-edged sword, of great value if used sensitively but capable also of creating tension and division.

We feel that these are important issues which all schools have to address, but in particular it perhaps has more bearing on schools with a religious foundation. Certainly the effect of nurturing children in a particular framework of belief can be seen to have a fundamental significance for the child's developing worldview and it is something all those involved with children should be aware of and alerted to when considering the education of the whole child.

Section Three

The implications of the research

10 The implications for education

Clive Erricker

What is the significance of children's storying?

THE MINISTER FOR EXAMS

When I was a child I sat an exam.
The test was so simple
There was no way I could fail.

Q 1. Describe the taste of the moon.

It tastes like Creation I wrote,
It has the flavour of starlight.

Q 2. What colour is Love?

Love is the colour of the water a man
lost in the desert finds, I wrote.

Q 3. Why do snowflakes melt?

I wrote, they melt because they fall
onto the warm tongue of God.

There were other questions.
They were as simple.

I described the grief of Adam when he was expelled from
Eden.
I wrote down the exact weight of an elephant's dream.

Yet, today, many years later,
for my living I sweep the streets
or clean out the toilets of the fat hotels.

Why? Because I constantly failed my exams.
Why? Well let me set a test.

Q 1. How large is a child's imagination?
Q 2. How shallow is the soul of the Minister for Exams?

(Brian Patten)

In Patten's poem we are alerted to the distinction between two sorts of learning. He identifies the fact that a concentration on received knowledge can retard children's development in other directions and that the outcome of this can be disempowerment and disaffection. Equally, our research has pointed to the need for children to be enabled to express and reflect on learning derived from experience and imagination. This is not secondary to or entirely distinct from their capacity to respond to identifiable knowledge targets within the curriculum. The development of children's language and ideas is enriched by reflection on life experiences, especially where these have been significant, as with death, loss, conflict and separation. It is also enriched by imaginatively playing with ideas concerning their relationship with and place in the world. In this way they engage affectively with metaphysical, moral, social and existential concerns which lie at the heart of education and which the curriculum itself must seek to address. Together, these two areas of children's learning, though not entirely distinct from one another, constitute two types of narrative that children construct in order to confer meaning on what would otherwise be a chaotic world. The result of ignoring children's needs in these respects is that they may feel isolated and anxious in relation to the experiences they have undergone, and undervalued in terms of their opinions and the contribution they have to make to the resolution of problems. They may also regard their imaginative thinking as insignificant in relation to what is considered to be 'real' (i.e. factual) knowledge, emphasized as the means to raising academic standards.

The reason for the problems which the children featured in Chapter 7 encountered in dealing with the loss issues is that they had not been given any basis or help in constructing an imaginative narrative to confer meaning on these difficult experiences and to give them a place in the framework of their understanding – to allow them to make sense of them. This process is illustrated by the way in which P constructs a story to explain the death of her grandfather. It can also be shown in the way in which V's grandmother constructs the story for her and encourages her to play imaginatively with the scenario and to gain ownership of the ideas and therefore place them in her own framework of experience and understanding.

Thus, in the case of V and her grandmother, it underpins and retrieves their relationship for V and posits its future continuance. Such stories also underpin and cohere explanations of other relationships, such as those with animals, and frame a view of the world that confirms certain attitudes and distinguishes between right and wrong actions. Given this, storying operates as purposeful myth; that is, a narrative that provides the foundation for doctrine, morality and social convention. Its primary aim is to order the world by identifying the classification of things such as relationships and rights, upon which notions of justice are founded. Myth is continually challenged by the notion of progress, which is justified through claims to more advanced knowledge. Our adjudication of these claims is the basis on which we determine the value of our present mythology. This is a complex process because shifts in knowledge are like small steps forward but changes in mythology are paradigm shifts, a complete altering of perspective. We are never in a position where the former fully resolves itself in the latter. However, by employing a historical perspective we can identify a sense of direction, the direction we should take, and in this resides our hope for the future. As a result our mythological perspective changes, we jettison what we think we no longer require and retain what we consider valuable. Just as we regularly undertake the clearing out of unwanted items from our house, so we do the same with our minds and our society. Equally we sometimes regret what we have thrown out and may attempt to retrieve it.

Children are continually involved in this process because of the rapidity with which change occurs in their lives. As adults, we can regard this simply as the process of development which we seek to monitor, influence and bring to fruition. One day, hopefully, they will become as mature as us and their mythologies and informed opinions will be worth taking account of, provided that they have developed well. This understanding makes sense if we think of education in curriculum terms as the acquisition of knowledge, but not if we see children as partners in the development of our mythology. After all, they are the recipients of our values as well as what we think constitutes our progress. And, as we have witnessed in the evidence of the preceding chapters in this book, they are already engaged in the sense-making activities of being human with which we continue to wrestle.

Given this, we have to recognize that education is constructed on one of two differing theoretical bases. The first is what we might call the 'received wisdom' model, in which power, authority and knowledge are communicated downwards in a hierarchically descending order, starting with governmental prescription and terminating with pupils. In this model, instruction takes precedence over development and knowledge is identified as an end-product rather than the ongoing and ever-changing result of open-ended enquiry. The intention of such an approach is to create a society that reflects this educational structure: ordered, convergent, doctrinally rigid. It denies the value of plurality, the provisionality of 'truth' and the ongoing search for meaning. It therefore denigrates the role that children can play in their own and society's development.

We might call the second model the 'developmental' model, in which learning and knowledge are seen as developing through a process of communication between different interest groups, children being one, parents another, faith communities a third, and academic and scientific 'communities' representing others. The aim in this model is not to agree as to what are undeniable truths and fictions but to be partners in learning and enrichment; these being the prerequisites for social and educational progress. The object of the exercise is not to arrive at truth but to communicate 'truths' or 'worldviews'.

Given this, we should recognize that stories which children tell are inherently unfalsifiable; i.e. they are true if you believe them, in which case their status is derived from their plausibility. Plausibility is established according to how far the story functions as an enabling or empowering explanation of experience. We can ignore the issue of whether the 'story' is 'true' and that allows us to consider its value in terms of its function, rather than being caught up in vexed questions as to how we determine the truth of people's stories. This is not to say that we do not challenge the attitudes and explanations of the experiences that children provide, but that we negotiate and converse with them from our own perspective.

The issue of respect

Ensuring that we listen to, converse with and take account of children's storying significantly influences our idea of education and the assumptions we make about the value of the thinking of children. It also vitally affects what we are inclined to call citizenship as an investment in the future quality of adult life.

The pay-off for the sort of investment we are suggesting is not a supplement to children's learning, which can be provided if there are sufficient funds. This places it in much the same category as we presently regard the Welfare State. Rather, we are arguing for an underpinning of our educational provision, such that it is properly contextualized within our vision of future society. If we can accept that knowledge is gained from experience and that it is communicated and refined through reflective conversation with others, then we have constructed an aim that should be embedded in every school policy. But first we have to agree that this kind of knowledge, what we might call 'life knowledge', cannot be developed catechetically through the imposition of another's truth upon the child. It might be argued that the above conversations do occur between children and teachers and that they also occur outside of school, with other adults, in families and other social groups where the child is taken into account. But if such an argument were voiced for the justification of not including a particular subject in the curriculum we would decry it. If we take this responsibility as seriously as any other, in educational terms, it cannot be left to serendipity or the open possibility of its occurring somewhere else in the child's experience. Like any other educational venture, it requires intervention, planning and close attention to implementation and monitoring. At issue is how this can best be done. The clues come from the children themselves. Every school is different in the sense that the children constitute a different overall character commensurate with its catchment area. Each school must take account of this. The example of the school which served Asian children is the most obvious in this respect. However, it would be a false presumption to think that only certain schools have need of such provision. We seem to have developed a false impression that children in some areas and with certain social backgrounds are in need, while others are not. The comments from the headteachers and teachers of the various schools we have worked in are indicative of this not being the case.

Further evidence of the need for provision can be derived from the children themselves. In the studies we have undertaken we have noted how the effect of significant experiences has altered those children's capacity to think in mature and realistic ways about themselves and their relationships with others. This sometimes manifests itself in their ability to deal with situations which offer the first taste of mortality. At other times it constitutes dealing with situations which require coming to terms with events that they do not have the power to rectify. We have also illustrated how children can engage in the discussion of difficult moral problems and arrive at mature and reasoned conclusions by drawing on their own experiences, and cite religious and scientific authority in discussing metaphysical issues. Furthermore, children have shown how they are able to construct notions of identity based upon their social and religious experiences. These findings indicate not only the richness of children's lives and capabilities, which we largely fail to exploit in the development of their own learning, but also just how relevant to the curriculum these issues are.

Why, then, do we so often fail to recognize and utilize children's thinking? The answer would seem to be embedded in the way we devise the curriculum itself, and this reflects the tendency we have to rely on the first of the educational models referred to above. It is both more difficult and risky to devise a curriculum that places the development of children's thinking and learning at its heart. It involves schools in sensitive negotiation with parents and demands more of teachers in terms of their time and the skills required. It also redefines their role and the way in which curriculum content is balanced with the acquisition of skills. Furthermore, it demands that attitudes be centrally addressed in the context of learning, since learning must be perceived as a corporate endeavour in which we learn from one another. As every teacher knows, this is the most difficult balance to maintain, since it mirrors the very problem that society itself faces. It is the greatest hindrance to both learning in the classroom and social progress. Furthermore, society's whole perception of the role of children would have to change: the role of children's function in society as traditionally understood. Adults have always retained authority and with that the idea that they have superior intelligence and potential. Children do not necessarily have less capability but it is simply that their abilities are different from those desired in adulthood.

This, of course, takes us to the heart of the problem: there are also political reasons, beyond the locality of individual schools and teachers interacting with their class, which cause the 'received wisdom' model to predominate in the way that education, curriculum and schooling are conceived and implemented. This is the sub-text of Patten's poem quoted at the beginning of this chapter.

The current battleground, in this respect, is the initiative related to SCMS (spiritual, cultural, moral and social) development. At present it is ill-defined, but there are two dangers: first, it will be an *ad hoc* addition to the curriculum which both schools and inspectors will regard as of secondary importance; second, it will become a political tool for ensuring the inculcation of values commensurate with social policy. In neither of these respects does it advantage children's learning and yet it is the means whereby children's experience can best be acknowledged in the context of their learning, given the present model of education.

Observations based on our own research and that of others, notably Wells (1986), Sacks (1985), Sontag (1991), Coles (1992) and Usher (1994) along with Ward (1995), Leaman (1995), Jewett (1994) and Meek *et al.* (1977) suggest that our present model does not sufficiently accommodate children's capacities to learn and as a result both retards their development and marginalizes academic underachievers. An event related by Coles is particularly apt in this respect.

Coles had tried, unsuccessfully, to interview Hopi (Indian) children in their school. It was the cleaner – herself a Hopi – who alerted him to the fact that they would not talk to him about themselves and their beliefs unless he spoke to them where they felt at home. As a result he went to talk with one of them where she lived, and the following conversation ensued.

On that first afternoon, when we really talked, we were sitting on chairs in front of her house. For miles beyond us stretched the flat desert – and then, abruptly, a mesa. Natalie [the girl he was interviewing] explains 'I think of the mesa a lot; it is where our people live, who are gone, and my mother was taken there when she was little, and she has taken me there, so I think a lot about the mesa, a lot. I visit it (in my thoughts) and I meet our ancestors ... I feel myself sometimes wanting to lift off, go right to the mesa and have a feast: eat our bread, stand in a circle, and hear my grandmother talk about our people.'   (Coles, 1992, pp. 149–50)

Psychologically – or metaphorically – speaking, every child has a mesa, or at least attempts to construct one. This is the landscape within which their existential reality is defined, which involves their relationships, both with the living and the dead, their concerns as to their present identity and their future aspirations, and, most important, it is the central location in their map of the world to which they can retreat, as a sanctuary, and from where they obtain their energy for living. Education, in its widest sense, is about affirming this sense of being, and schooling necessarily entails understanding it as the departure point and context of children's learning. Failing to do so will result in the curriculum being an irrelevance for most pupils unless they and their parents subscribe to its demands in relation to their desire for individual achievement and, possibly, social progress. In this case it will necessarily serve an 'academic', elitist minority.

Wells' research is interesting in respect of the above, since he cites that, with regard to language, children who do not usually produce complex structures indicating a more advanced level of intellectual functioning will 'occasionally produce utterances of this kind [which is] evidence that he or she can do so when he or she judges the situation to warrant it' (Wells, 1986, p. 127). This coincides with our research in which we have found that children, with no previous record of significant academic achievement, can relate, through metaphorical constructions, a deep understanding of their experiences. Wells comments further that the child's performance 'does not depend on ability alone, but on the complex interrelationship between the participants, the task, and the context in which it is embedded' (Wells, 1986, p. 126). Our research again concurs with these findings in that what children reveal, in relation to their thinking and experiences, depends on the degree of trust that they invest in those they are conversing with.

The threads of the reflections drawn together in this chapter amount to a plea for a more holistic, egalitarian and poetic view of education that balances rationalism with intuitive awareness, order with diversity and economic goals with social enrichment. After all, the health and vision of a society can only be achieved through addressing the health and vision of each of its members. A first step towards this can be made, in the words of one of the children interviewed by Coles, who said: 'The only chance for the nation to be united is that way, for kids to learn about other kids, for all kids to have that chance' (Coles, 1992, p. 159).

References

Coles, R. (1992) *The Spiritual Life of Children*. London, HarperCollins.

Jewett, C. (1994) *Helping Children Cope with Separation and Loss*. London, Batsford.

Leaman, O. (1995) *Death and Loss: Compassionate Approaches in the Classroom*. London, Cassell.

Meek, M., Warlow, A. and Barton, G. (eds) (1977) *The Cool Web: The Pattern of Children's Reading*. London, The Bodley Head.

Sacks, O. (1985) *The Man Who Mistook His Wife for a Hat*. London, Duckworth.

Sontag, S. (1991) *Illness As Metaphor and Aids and Its Metaphors*. Harmondsworth, Penguin.

Usher, R. (1994) *Postmodernism and Education*. London, Routledge.

Ward, B. (1995) *Good Grief: Exploring Feelings, Loss and Death with Under Elevens*. London, Jessica Kingsley.

Wells, G. (1986) *The Meaning Makers: Children Learning Language and Using Languages to Learn*. Portsmouth, Hodder & Stoughton.

11 The implications for the classroom

Jane Erricker and Clive Erricker

Introduction

What are the implications of this research for classroom teaching and learning? They are threefold.

- The first concerns the relationship between teacher and learner.
- The second concerns our aims as teachers in developing children's learning.
- The third concerns the relationship between curriculum attainment targets and content and child development.

Our argument is that these three considerations should be suitably balanced and that, at present, this is not the case. The pressures on teachers to fulfil National Curriculum targets is one obvious reason for this; another is the pressure in teacher training to deliver the formal curriculum, rather than to become skilful educators. The result is a myopic understanding of the professional role with no sense of educational vision. While this situation can only be fully addressed in the longer term it is possible to go about our task in a more enlightened way. The suggestions that follow can be understood as tools or strategies which the project has found useful and which, we believe, translate into the classroom situation. In doing so they help to address the implications mentioned above.

1. Concept mapping

In *Learning How to Learn* (1984), Novak and Gowin describe concept maps as 'intended to represent meaningful relationships between concepts in the form of propositions'. Put more simply, it can be understood as being an activity similar to but more structured than brainstorming. It can also be used as a follow-up activity to the latter. It is most often employed as a method of diagnostic and summative assessment. In other words, it can identify exactly what a child has learned from what has been taught in a particular subject, scheme of work or topic. In this situation the object is to measure children's learning according to teacher- and subject-led notions of knowledge. We first became aware of its more extensive value by using it in this way with one of our own children. Before taking part in a school topic on earth and space, P prepared a concept map at home based on the topic. A list of concepts was drawn up by asking her what words she thought of in relation to these terms. She was then asked to go through her list by writing down one of her words and connecting it to a second with a line. Then she had to write a statement beside the line explaining how the two terms were connected. The activity then followed the same pattern in connecting up all her words. The finished map is shown in Figure 11.1.

If we analyse the map what do we learn? Well, there are two ways of analysing it. One is according to Piagetian criteria, whereby we can identify that the child exhibits many of the characteristics of animistic thinking. Similar statements by children can be found in Piaget's work *A Child's Conception of the World* (1973). To do this would be to confirm what stage of development the child had reached. However, if we look differently at what P has written we can appreciate the poetry of her imaginative thinking, which conceives the world as a fascinating place that reveals the liveness of and relationship between things as she imagines them to be. It is not necessary to choose between the two modes of analysis. It is not a matter of which one is right and which wrong. They belong within different frames of reference. To use the former and dismiss the latter, however, would be reductionist. It would deny the imaginative and poetic capabilities of the child

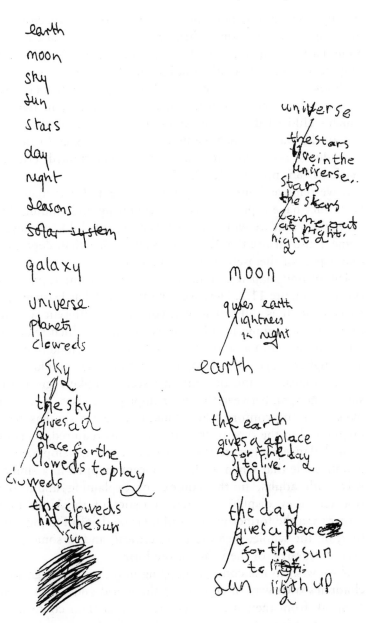

Figure 11.1   P's first concept map of earth and space

and by implication, our appreciation of those capacities in social and cultural terms. This, of course, relates back to the point Patten is making in the poem quoted in the previous chapter and to similar observations made by Oliver Sacks in his book *The Man Who Mistook His Wife for a Hat* (1985), in which he relates his neurological case studies, in two of which – Hildegard of Bingen and Rebecca – he raises the question of the way in which we judge the capacities and value of individuals according to our own predetermined criteria (Sacks, 1985, pp. 161–2, 175–7).

If we remove from the map the statements P has made we do in fact have a poem. It is by recognizing and valuing this as teachers that we will enhance this aspect of children's development and ensure that they appreciate rather than deprecate that aspect of themselves as they mature.

The second map was done after completing the topic. It is shown in Figure 11.2. Here we can see what P has learned and measure it. It is indicative of a completely different way of thinking conforming to different expectations which relate to different educational aims. It is possible to conclude that P is at a higher stage of development because her thinking no longer appears animistic, but this seems unlikely given the short time span between the two mapping exercises. It is more likely that she conforms her thinking to what she has been taught and to the type of thinking that was required. At issue is the balance we give to these two aspects of development. It is noticeable that when we have concept mapped in a similar way with adults, in the context of explaining about our research, they display the characteristics of the latter map rather than the former in terms of their mode of thinking, and that, on the whole, men are more critical, and in some cases even dismissive, of the value of the former.

If we wish to use concept mapping in order to engage with children's own way of conceiving the world and to ask them to speak from their own experience, rather than conform to our expectations, it can be a useful tool for focusing child-led discussion and reflection. It provides a structured task to focus

Figure 11.2 P's second concept map

but not inhibit their thinking, and can lead on to a guided discussion in which children can learn from each other. In this context they can come to appreciate the viewpoints and diverse ways of thinking that arise out of different social, cultural and religious experiences. They will enrich their own thinking, outlooks and values as a result, provided that we do not encumber them with our own inhibitions. They will appre-

149

ciate the 'how' of learning as well as the 'what'. This, of course, applies to the other techniques identified in this chapter.

2. Draw and Write

Draw and Write, or Drawing and Dialogue, is a technique for accessing an individual's ideas and has been used particularly in the area of health education. Theresa Shaver and her colleagues (Shaver *et al.,* 1993) have used the technique with adults to assess needs for health education planning in, for example, Africa, India and Fiji. Noreen Whetton and her colleagues (Williams *et al.,* 1989) have uncovered the perceptions of children concerning their health using Draw and Write, and this information has informed the design of health education programmes for primary schools.

As Theresa Shaver says, 'Experimenting with drawing and dialogue can provide a way of unlocking how people see and understand the world' (Shaver *et al.,* 1993, p. 1). Given a quote such as this, it is easy to see why the technique appealed to members of the project team as another way of revealing children's unique perceptions of the situations in which they find themselves.

We have not used the technique exactly as it is described by Noreen Whetton and her colleagues. In their work the real skill is the question that is asked in order to elicit the picture and the writing around it. In our inexperienced hands the technique has been far less subtle but has still shown the potential of drawing a picture and talking about it as a means of clarifying the artist's thought and communicating ideas to another.

The technique is simple. The child (or adult) is asked to draw a picture in response to a question and then either to write some words associated with the drawing, or to talk about the drawing. It is important that the drawing itself is not analysed in terms of, say, colours used or positioning of figures, but that it only serves as a focus of thoughts which are expressed orally or in writing. We found that, because the chil-

Figure 11.3   R's picture of heaven

dren we were researching were quite young, we usually talked about the drawings rather than wrote about them.

The drawings in Figures 11.3 to 11.5 were produced by 6-year-old children in the course of an interview which had produced a discussion about where we, and our pets, went when we died. The concept of heaven had been raised, and the

151

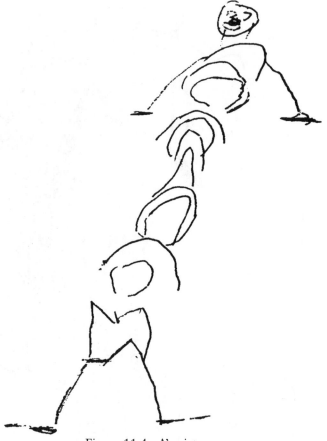

Figure 11.4 A's picture

interviewer wanted to ascertain more about the children's understanding of the nature of heaven. The children were asked to draw heaven and the results are illustrated here. But of course far more important is the dialogue that ensued after the drawings. More detail about the interviews in which these children participated can be found in Chapter 5.

Figure 11.3 is R's picture of heaven. The heaven that he drew was an alien planet, with the inhabitants waiting on the surface for dead animals to arrive. When they did arrive, the alien beings grabbed them and took them underground. This

I Think heven is like This so
Thats way I drew it

Figure 11.5 N's picture

heaven was not intended for human beings, just for animals.

In subsequent and previous discussions R showed his over-riding concern for animals and his scientific knowledge. He had had no overt religious nurture and his concept of heaven showed no influence of religious ideas. Heaven was 'up there' and 'up there' was space and stars and planets. His picture gave the interviewer more information about his concept and allowed him to explain in more detail.

Figure 11.4 was drawn by A. The picture is quite difficult to understand until it is explained in conversation. It is a skeleton because if you are dead you must be a skeleton. Again there is no obvious religious influence in the picture and none was revealed in the conversation about the picture, although this child did have a religious background.

Figure 11.5 was drawn by N. N needed some persuasion to draw at all. He was also capable of writing about his picture and he was encouraged to do so, but this took some effort. When he was asked to talk about his picture he explained that heaven was full of spirits and spirits were just thin air. As he could not draw thin air he drew a house for the interviewer. He wrote what he wrote again because he was asked to write. This example illustrates more than any other that the child must be talked to about the picture because it would have been easy to conclude that this child too had no religious concept of heaven. Instead the child had a very sophisticated concept which owed a great deal to his religious nurture, and it was only revealed by the conversation around the picture.

Just like concept mapping, this technique of drawing and conversation can be used to access ideas in all curriculum areas and reveals misconceptions both before and after teaching a particular area of knowledge and understanding. In this sense it is a useful tool for assessment.

3. Interviewing

Interviewing is the name we gave to talking to groups or pairs of children in the project's research, but at times we were talking to 60 children in an assembly and recording what they said, or to a class of between 15 and 30. We came to realize that it was not necessary to divide children into small groups to initiate discussion related to their own experience and views, even though one might want to follow up in this way or arrange separate meetings afterwards. A better title in the classroom context might therefore be 'structured discussion' based on a theme or relevant issue. The important preparation for this is twofold: ensuring the necessary provision is possible if it leads into extra curricular needs (see Chapters 8 and 9), and understanding what techniques, strategies and resources a teacher will need to employ in order to facilitate and manage such discussions. This section addresses the latter, which can be identified as follows:

- choosing an appropriate initial stimulus;
- using open questions;
- listening and responding to significant contributions;
- raising issues that will encourage further reflection;
- being sensitive to the 'mood' or atmosphere of the group and that of individuals within it;
- being self-aware of any tendency to promote a particular outcome.

What follows addresses putting these into operation.

The initial stimulus needs to address concerns that engage with the children's experience and interest. It also needs to have depth in the sense that it deals with questions of meaning and value. As a first example we can refer back to Chapter 4 and the poem 'Looking for Dad'. Here the story-line is about a young boy, his room and his parents; the underlying concept is that of loss. The children's responses to it are various, but the important issue to bear in mind is to identify when a child signals that he or she has engaged with the concept at an experiential level. This requires that we do not insist on talking about the situation in the poem but seek to allow the children to relate it to themselves in whatever way is meaningful for them. In other words, we follow the concept, not the story-line. In order to do this we must employ a particular questioning technique, that of asking open questions, to prompt children's responses. This allows us to identify when a child has engaged with the concept in the way mentioned above. At this point the ensuing discussion will centre around such responses and our task, as the facilitator, is to ensure that our interventions guide what has now become the children's collective storying, and to clarify issues that may arise. The aim is that children should learn from other children in the context of the discussion, not that it should have a prescribed outcome, in terms of the views children should hold. This does not mean that anything goes, but it does mean that we must be as aware as possible of any subliminal tendencies on our part to bias children's thinking toward a particular point of view when other opinions they express might be just as valid. The key is to maintain the quality of the learning process, which also means sensitively directing the discussion away from animosity, but not avoiding the expression of contrary opinion. It is also important to establish certain ground rules concerning sensitivity towards and valuing others, speaking in turn, and when a discussion should be ended. It is valuable to actually tape record discussions, as long as this is agreed by everyone. This helps to ensure that, by passing the tape recorder around, everyone is aware of whose turn it is to speak. It also emphasizes the importance attached to what a child has to say. Finally, it can also provide further initial stimulus for subsequent 'meetings'. We have found that children responding to other children is a most valuable process. The stimulus itself, of course, can be anything with the qualities we described above: a question, an object, a picture, a story. What matters is the way it is used, which is, of course, at the heart of all good teaching and learning. This process is not just an exercise in developing 'philosophical thinking'. Learning to reason effectively is also a part of it. But the appreciation of the experiences and worldviews of others and the enrichment of one's own is the more significant aim, and it is only by engaging with the affective domain that we can bring this about and understand the relevance of learning to our lives. We need to be aware that this can be an uncomfortable experience, especially for the teacher. It means giving up a certain sense of authority on which we may rely. It also means risking certain outcomes we cannot predict, and often struggling to direct situations that we cannot stand back from and assess. This is all unavoidable, as we have found on the project. But, in the long run, we believe that it is beneficial for all concerned.

Conclusion

It is justifiable to ask how the strategies outlined above can best be utilized in relation to the curriculum we are required to teach. More is said about this in the concluding chapter of the book where we consider the relationship between prescribed content and children's learning. Nevertheless, it is possible to reflect on the relationship between teaching styles and the delivery of knowledge and understanding in order to ask how the two can best be married. We can teach didactically in order to convey information most effectively. We can employ experiential learning strategies to engage the learner more effectively. By utilizing the idea of narrative learning we may deliver the curriculum content in such a way that the learner can immediately engage with it. By narrative learning we mean that the subject matter must be conveyed in such a way that the historical, social, cultural, artistic or religious experience involved is prevalent in the delivery, which then allows the learner to respond, using his or her imagination and experience to do so. This implies that our own knowledge and the resources we use must be adapted accordingly. Illustrations of how this might be accomplished can be found in the chapters on religious education and collective worship (Chapter 12) and children's spirituality and our contemporary culture (Chapter 13).

Concept mapping, Draw and Write and interviewing are all methods of accessing children's ideas and are therefore methods of formative assessment. They all allow us to identify the starting point for our teaching, the framework of ideas and experiences that a child has constructed so far in his or her life. They also allow us to monitor the changes in that framework which occur as a result of our teaching. We are therefore able to identify misconceptions that arise because of a mismatch between our teaching methods and a child's learning. The curriculum is something taught, but it is also something learned, and if we bring our own experiences and those of others in story form to the children by communicating experience rather than just fact, the children are much better able to respond with their own feelings and reflections. We are the bridge between knowledge and understanding: the former relates to what we teach, the latter to what children learn. If we are to deliver the curriculum the balance must be maintained, and therefore the strategies we employ have to be equally weighted between the didactic and the affective. Before we can help children to enter into this process we must go through it ourselves and relate it to our own experience; otherwise we cannot be successful in our own recognition of the task.

References

Novak, J.D. and Gowin, D.B. (1984) *Learning How to Learn.* Cambridge, Cambridge University Press.

Piaget, J. (1973) *A Child's Conception of the World.* St Albans, Paladin.

Sacks, O. (1985) *The Man Who Mistook His Wife for a Hat.* London, Duckworth.

Shaver, T., Francis, V. and Barnett, L. (1993) *Drawing as Dialogue: A Qualitative Approach to Needs Assessment for Health Education Planning.* Education Resource Group, Liverpool School of Tropical Medicine.

Williams, T., Whetton, N. and Moon, A. (1989) *A Picture of Health: What Do You Do That Makes You Healthy and Keeps You Healthy?* Health Education Authority, UK.

12 Religious education and collective worship

Danny Sullivan and Clive Erricker

Religious education

It was noted in Chapter 2 that when the first draft of the National Curriculum was published mathematics, English and science were seen to be the all-important areas of the curriculum and learning. This has subsequently been challenged, though very often the reality remains that the focus is on the core areas of the curriculum. The politicization of education makes it difficult to have a reasoned debate about curriculum content and time.

While there is no space here to rehearse the full history of the development of religious education in England and Wales it could be claimed that, in fact, it has been circular rather than linear. It would appear that within religious education we return to familiar debates and struggles without really resolving key issues. For example, in 1944 the Butler Act gave us religious instruction and, while the 1988 Education Reform Act changed this to religious education, there remained strident calls for children to be instructed in the Ten Commandments and the Lord's Prayer in their religious education lessons.

Despite the best efforts of RE advisers and notable bodies like the Christian Education Movement (CEM), the Shap Working Party on World Religions in Education, the Professional Council for Religious Education and the Religious Education Council for England and Wales, the progress of religious education can remain patchy and inconsistent. In primary schools, there appear to be a variety of

159

criteria for appointing teachers to the role of RE co-ordinator and resourcing of the subject remains woefully low compared to other curriculum areas. Teacher training institutions have found the time available for preparing students to teach RE ever more restricted, as mathematics, English and science and the agenda of OFSTED take hold. In a four-year programme, students can have as little as 20 to 30 hours of professional RE, which may lead to their entering schools as newly quali- fied teachers only to find very little RE anyway or a deep nervousness about it. RE syllabuses and programmes often celebrate the fact that in engaging in the religious quest we can discover through all the major religious traditions how they respond to the ultimate questions of life: Who am I? Why am I on this earth? Will there be life after death? Robert Coles expresses this evocatively in his book *The Spiritual Life of Children* when he writes:

> So it is we connect with one another, move in and out of one another's lives, teach and heal and affirm one another, across space and time – all of us wanderers, explorers, adventurers, stragglers, and ramblers, sometimes tramps or vagabonds, even fugitives, but now and then pilgrims: as children, as parents, as old ones about to take that final step, to enter that territory whose character none of us here ever knows. Yet how young we are when we start wondering about it all, the nature of the journey and of the final destination.
> (Coles, 1992, p. 335)

Throughout the project, we have rarely found a school or class teacher who was unsympathetic to the nurture of this dimension within children. Yet loyal, hard-working and dedi- cated teachers wonder where they are to find the time not only to empower their pupils to become fully human and alive, but also to free themselves to be so. Furthermore, they are often unsure how to bring together teaching about religions and developing children's own personal enquiry. The demands of a crowded curriculum, the pressure and politicization of inspections and league tables, the constant maligning of and carping at teachers can leave professional people feeling deeply uncertain and insecure about their real skills and qualities. It is a sad commentary on the point we have reached in our society that it takes horrific incidents and tragedies like the murders of headteacher Philip Lawrence and the innocent 5-year-olds in Dunblane to bring home to some people in politics and in the media the scale of the human and pastoral qualities that teachers bring to their schools and classrooms every day.

Like music, art and drama, RE has often had to fight for its very soul and survival, even in the post-Dearing curriculum. On the positive side, many schools (church and county) have remained fully committed to the place of RE and have given it due time and resourcing. In a paradoxical sense, OFSTED inspections have meant that schools will be expected to have a policy and programme for RE, a co-ordinator and reasonable resourcing. The HMI responsible for RE has stated that this has begun to have a positive effect in schools and that RE is at last beginning to be taken seriously. However, this is as yet a long way from guaranteeing a quality of experience in this key area of development for all children. If RE becomes, like other subjects, too content-led, we remain in danger of continuing to miss the real lives and experiences of children. The children in the project consistently remind us of many real and deep experiences they encounter. These experiences speak to them as full human beings, whether they are finding their own sacred space or dealing frankly and openly with their feelings about a bereavement or the breakup of their parents' relationship. If in our fear of the inspection or the league table – really our fear of failing – we abandon the effective education of the children in our schools, what kind of harvest might we be reaping for them and indeed for ourselves?

RE needs a content. Children need to be taken seriously. If children are to have the confidence to engage in ultimate questions through RE, then teachers as adult human beings need to discover a confidence of allowing that to happen in their own lives. There is a danger with a syllabus which is over-focused on content (be it an LEA, a diocesan or a SCAA Model Syllabus) that it will lead to a teaching *about* religions, rather than an engaging with the heart of a religion. We do not have to believe in or accept the values of a tradition, but we can learn to respect that tradition and the followers who take it to their hearts. Religious communities need to trust to schools and teachers and recognize – in state schools – the difference between a faith community and an educational community. If religion is taken as an opportunity to withdraw or separate our children from particular traditions, then once again the needs and rights of children can be overlooked or lost altogether.

There is much to celebrate in the progress and development of resources for RE material, such as *A Gift to the Child* (Grimmitt *et al.*, 1991), which allows children a stimulating and involving insight into the religious life of their peers. Programmes from faith communities, such as *Here I Am* from the Roman Catholic community, have endeavoured to take seriously how children grow and develop in their primary years. In *Here I Am* (Byrne and Malone, 1992), children are taken through a process which recognizes among other things their right to reflect and to rejoice in the very best sense of those words. The curriculum materials produced by the Warwick Religious Education and Community Project also provide valuable resources for first school RE based on ethnographic enquiry.

Thus there is no lack of resources available to engage children with those very real experiences they meet in their everyday lives. Deep down there is no lack of belief and commitment among teachers that children and teachers need and have the right to develop every aspect of their humanity. However, there is a lack of vision and belief among those who would oversee education that this whole area of human experience and formation is critical to our children's future. A radical reappraisal is needed of what religious education can contribute to the lives of our schools and classrooms and a bold courage to discover a sense of authentic vision and direction.

With this in mind, we must recognize that what is taught is

not some 'thing'. For example, Islam or Christianity is found in the lives of religious communities and can be identified in the utterances of believers. Surrounding this and informing it is what we may call the 'tradition'. The tradition is not something distinct from the communities in which it is embodied. Nobody speaks for it but those who belong to those communities. Recognizing this has implications for our teaching and pupils' learning. The first issue it raises is representation. As teachers, we wish to represent a tradition faithfully, but this can be reduced to simply acquainting children with its beliefs and practices as though they 'speak for themselves'. The impression then given is that there are religious people of various persuasions who, belonging to the same tradition, all believe in the same thing without struggle or question. Such people do not exist. Children know this, and therefore the result of such an approach is to depersonalize the subject through stereotypical representation, however 'accurate' or 'orthodox' that representation is. The second issue is politicization. To bring the subject alive and make it relevant to children's learning it has to be politicized. This word can send shudders through us all, but let us explain the particular meaning we wish to give to it. No individual 'accurately' represents a tradition or a community; he or she can only represent him or herself. This is the case even if that individual is invested with the authority to represent others. Thus, where such representation occurs it necessarily becomes a matter of debate within the community. An obvious example relates to the role and pronouncements of the Pope in Christianity and Catholicism, but the same issues arise across religion generally and in other non-religious contexts. It is important to focus on the debate and the issues being debated. This is what we mean by politicization.

As a result, RE becomes process-oriented and skills-based. The subject matter is to be determined on the basis of being appropriately illustrative. What we are seeking to do is engage the learner with fundamental issues that pertain to being human which religions have investigated, but which relate to

163

non-religious worldviews as well as religious ones. Our aim is to help children develop their own worldviews, within whatever social and religious context pertains, and to engage with the worldviews of others. To argue that what has been outlined above is beyond children, especially young children, is to ignore the evidence presented throughout this book. The key to achieving this is to engage with the children's own ideas and experiences and to recognize that 'worldviews' is not a term for coherent and systematically held doctrines, beliefs and values rationally packaged, but an umbrella term within which we investigate the sense-making derived from the use of our rational, emotional and intuitive intelligence applied to our own experience and the experience of others.

As a result of this approach, children will come to understand the 'language' of religion as expressed through ritual, visual and verbal or written expression because its function will be apprehended by virtue of reflecting on the way in which the same forms of expression are used by them to explicate and communicate their own experience, as we have seen in the course of the studies in this book.

The next step is to ascertain the structure of this approach as far as the children's learning is concerned. What exactly will the children be doing when they are engaged in religious education? Initially, the aim will be to concentrate on the children's own experiences, and the teacher's role will be to allow the temporal and psychological space for children to express these experiences without fear of judgement either by the teacher or by peers. The sharing of the issues arising from their experiences will result in reflection and a deeper understanding of what is being addressed, still within the context of the worldviews of the children in a particular class, which are being expressed within the narratives that they tell. With the skills of identification of the issues and reflection on those issues introduced and to some extent developed, it is possible to apply them to the subject matter of the curriculum, which can then be addressed at a deeper level. This amounts to an engagement of minds rather than simply an apprehension of outward forms and descriptions. In summary, this process can be described as identification, reflection and application.

Collective worship

It would be true to say that the section of the 1988 Act on collective worship caused much more anxiety and unease than did the section on religious education. The language relating to collective worship seemed much more presumptuous and even imposing than had been felt for a long time. Some teachers in county schools understandably felt nervous about providing an act of worship which was 'mainly or broadly of a Christian character'. The section on collective worship bears all the hallmarks of something which has been produced in some haste and, sadly, without any detailed consideration of responses from the consultation process. Confusion abounds. The word 'worship' is to be understood by its normal, ordinary meaning, but collective worship must not relate to any particular denomination. By agreement between parents and headteacher, it is permissible for a pupil to be present at collective worship, but not to take part. How do you explain that to a 5-year-old?

We suspect that some of these confusions arose because those who most strongly influenced this section of the Act were seeing collective worship as a means of improving the moral character and fibre of our children and therefore our society. While it is a perfectly valid desire to improve the moral character of society, we have to question whether legislation about the content of collective worship is the appropriate way to do this. In a paradoxical way, people who belong to a faith community ultimately make a free choice to do so. There will be an expectation of participating in the life of the faith community, but no compulsion. Today, many people who define their identity in religious terms do not necessarily feel the need to join regularly with a worshipping community. Mainstream churches have witnessed the development of house and community churches which seem keen to be much more free and flexible in their approach to faith and worship. Many young people and young adults are much attracted to the secular for a spirituality; hence, for example, the interest in Celtic Christianity and New Age ideas. Within major denominations such as the Anglican and Roman Catholic churches there has been a growing recognition of the specific needs and rights of children in terms of their religious and spiritual development. Robert Coles' book *The Spiritual Life of Children* (1992) bears testimony to the astonishing range of spiritual experiences which children encounter.

This makes it all the more disappointing that the legislation on collective worship takes no account of the range of developments in our understanding of religious belief and spirituality between 1944 and 1988. Furthermore, in drawing up the legislation someone has confused quantity with quality. All schools – church and county – are legally obliged to provide collective worship every day of the week. This is something that faith communities could desire, but it is interesting that they do not require it.

Recognizing this quantitative approach, one begins to appreciate the pressures teachers feel. Delivery of an overcrowded curriculum, inspections, SATs, league tables, collective worship five times a week – it is no wonder that the early exit rate from the teaching profession is higher than it has ever been. In county schools, teachers who are not religious or who are open-minded about the whole field of religious enquiry are very uncomfortable with the language of the 1988 legislation on collective worship. Inspections of schools have led to evidence that some schools which have broken the law by not providing daily collective worship are yet providing quality experiences for their pupils. On the other hand, some schools which were slavishly adhering to the legislation were providing experiences of poor quality.

What the legislation on collective worship betrays is a lack of trust in schools and in teachers and a wish to ensure traditional order based on religious and moral conformism. Guidelines and parameters could have been provided which, in the first instance, built upon the many examples of good practice to be found in both county and church schools. Where educationalists in church communities have recognized the variety of experience and background among the children in their schools, by contrast the legislation on collective worship for county schools appears to lump all children together as if they are the same. Again it is an opportunity lost.

Professor John Hull in an address to headteachers in the Anglican Diocese of Oxford in April 1996 defined spiritual education as that which inspires children to the service of others. Impeaching, or even debating, that definition could lead to a realistic yet stimulating and imaginative sense of how we might reflect this in schools.

Our work with children in our project has convinced us that teachers and pupils have a right to time to explore what it means to be human, to be religious, to be spiritual. However, to provide that time there needs to be a belief in the holistic education of children. In education, we need to have the courage to consider whether we have gone too far down the road of prescription and narrow expectation. By focusing the minds of teachers on what they are compelled to deliver in collective worship daily, have we missed tapping into a rich vein of creativity and imagination? There will be those who will argue that before 1988 there was such a disregard for collective worship that something had to be done. We would simply argue that the 1988 legislation is no guarantee of an improvement. This returns us to the thrust of much that we have discovered in the project. Can we begin to re-create our schools as human communities where children and adults can discover what it is to be in the very fullest sense?

As in families, so in schools, children can often provide the lead by commenting on their own experiences, as long as we don't explain them away as immature. An example of this has been provided in Chapter 8. We are forced to reflect on what we stifle rather than liberate. What might significant objectives for collective worship be? The following could be regarded as pointers in the right direction:

- the creation of community
- the sharing of authority
- a sense of belonging
- a vision of a common humanity
- reflection on that which transcends the everyday, immediate and material.

References

Byrne, A. and Malone, C. (1992) *Here I Am: A Religious Education Programme for Primary Schools.* London: HarperCollinsReligious.

Coles, R. (1992) *The Spiritual Life of Children.* London, HarperCollins.

Grimmitt, M., Grove, J., Hull, J.M. and Spencer, L. (1991) *A Gift to the Child: Religious Education in the Primary School* (Teachers' source book). Hemel Hempstead, Simon & Schuster.

Warwick Project: *Bridges to Religions,* Key Stage 1 (1995), Key Stage 2 (1996). Oxford, Heinemann.

13 Children's spirituality and our contemporary culture

Danny Sullivan

The 1988 Education Reform Act laid great stress on the importance of the spiritual, moral, social and cultural development of all pupils in our schools. Section 9 inspections by OFSTED have to report on the quality of this provision when they visit schools. However, detailed study on inspection reports would indicate that this area receives the briefest of attention, and often the four areas can be put together. This is worthy of note, since this aspect of pupil development is included in Part 1 of the Act, with the National Curriculum making up Part 2. Furthermore, the reality is that all the attention has been focused on the National Curriculum with little space or time given to the spiritual, moral, social and cultural aspects. When attention is paid to this side of pupil development confusion can still arise, with, for example, some commentators still speaking as if spirituality and morality were one and the same thing. Nick Tate, Chief Executive of SCAA, in calling for more teaching on morality, seemed to fall victim to this sense of muddle. He displayed a distinct lack of awareness of just how much teachers try to engage with the spiritual, moral, social and cultural. He confounded this muddled approach by later suggesting that if schools now had more leeway with curriculum time after Dearing they should think of bringing Latin and Greek back into place. Teachers do despair because of being constantly instructed about what to do with every minute of the school day and not being trusted to be imaginative or creative in their own right.

The danger in a narrow and prescriptive approach to learning and the curriculum is that we will yet again miss out on the opportunities to gain insight from what children bring to our schools and classrooms. They will remain persuaded that the thoughts, feelings, ideas and excitement of their inner lives and world are not for sharing with others – particularly adults. Through the project we have learned to respect this inner life and world of children and have come to see it as deeply spiritual in the widest possible sense. And yes, this spirituality has connected them to a sense of morality as the use of story has shown.

'Somewhere inside me the jasmine continues to blossom'

Etty Hillesum was a young Jewish woman who, like so many Jews, found herself in a concentration camp during the Second World War. She kept diaries, just as did Anne Frank, though Hillesum's diaries were only discovered in the 1980s. Her diaries reflect a person of remarkable resilience and a spirit who knew the fate which awaited her – she died in the camp. She retained a belief that, however awful the outer world which confronted her and her fellow Jews, there was an inner world, an inner space which could not be captured or taken away by anyone.

Thus she wrote in her diaries:

> The jasmine behind my house has been completely ruined by the rain and storms of the last few days; its white blossoms are floating about in muddy black pools on the low garage roof. But somewhere inside me the jasmine continues to blossom undisturbed, just as profusely and delicately as it ever did.
>
> I bring you not only my tears and my forebodings on this stormy, grey Sunday morning, I even bring you my scented jasmine. Even if I should be locked up in a narrow cell and a cloud should drift past my small window then I shall bring you that cloud, oh God, while there is still the strength in me to do so.
>
> (Hillesum, 1984, p. 188)

Etty Hillesum gives voice to the potential within all of us to confront the harsh realities of life at times and yet maintain an inner peace and balance. Such an approach to our world and everyday concerns and struggles would be echoed by those from all religious traditions and also those from no religious tradition at all. It is something to do with the essence of the human spirit and the capacity of human beings to rise above the most challenging situations and environments. Young children, as much as adults, have this capacity. They move in and out of different worlds. They have the capacity to adapt to and cope with the world of adults while at the same time protecting an inner world which fascinates and enthrals them. Violet Madge in her book *Children in Search of Meaning* (1965) described the children she worked with thus:

> A sense of mystery often accompanies the exercise of curiosity and there seem occasions when the mysteries may cause children to become conscious of eternal realities beyond phenomena.

Madge is writing about the children we meet in the ordinary day-to-day life of the classroom: those children who can drive us to distraction as well as inspire us with their insights and awareness; those children to whom we have to deliver all manner of curriculum and who discover within themselves varieties of attainments and level descriptors. Yet these very same children have deep inner reserves and a capacity to show to us and teach us things we, as adults, have perhaps long forgotten. This is not to glorify or idealize childhood or children but simply to remind us that, as Etty Hillesum shows, there are many layers to the human condition and spirit.

Working within a group of children

Over a considerable period of time I worked with a group of children from a Roman Catholic school. The school, being a church school, was served by a wide catchment area and thus the children came from a variety of backgrounds. There were parents from comfortable backgrounds. There were parents who struggled with the realities of unemployment. Pupils at church schools reflect our contemporary society in their family make-up and this was also reflected within the group. One boy in particular had seen a variety of male adults pass through his relatively short life. The school is warm, friendly and welcoming and there is a clear commitment to the well-being of the children. There is a contemporary religious education programme which teachers plan and prepare together. All teachers see it as a central aspect of the life of the school. Close links are maintained with the local parishes and with parents.

Hallowed ground

The first exploration with the group was to establish if they had a special place where they retreated to, and if so what was it that made it special. Within school we often ask children to explore this concept, though perhaps we do not always have the time to dig deeply with them as to their thoughts and feelings about their special and/or secret places. John Bowker (1993) in the chapter 'Remembered places' from his book *Hallowed Ground* describes this concept of space and place in the following way:

> The poetry of place, therefore, has the power to make us, not simply travellers in space, but travellers in time as well. It creates the possibility of our healing and our hope – first because it renews the days of our peace; but second also, because it can take us back to the places of our hurt in the past, and there, through the cleansing of our memory, it can start the process of our completion and cure. In that way it creates in us a better chance by far of becoming a hood of care and protection for others.

When we explored special places, S told us that he found the garage a good place to escape to, somewhere he could find something to do but where he didn't have to think. Notice that he *escapes* to the garage. Children, just like adults, have a desire and need to escape from the stresses and strains of life. As Bowker pointed out, places often have a poetry all of their own which enable us to reflect and think through aspects of our life. Not so for S. He simply wants to be, to do something practical and release his mind from thinking about whatever it is he has escaped from.

J simply went under her bed when she wanted space. The most important aspect of this was not to let on to others that she was there and she filled her time either by 'thinking about things' or 'playing little games in my head'. Again, we have the sense that she was taking control of her world and by retreating to her own private place she was giving herself the clear message that she had the right and freedom to opt into her world. Margaret Donaldson (1976) in *Children's Minds* comments: 'They can learn to be conscious of the powers of their own minds and decide to what ends they will use them' (p. 256).

T escaped into the wardrobe in his bedroom. Here it was dark and secret and he felt free. No fear of the dark, no fear of being enclosed. Absolute freedom to think, to be himself, to have a break from others, were the feelings he vigorously expressed.

The two remaining children had trees for their special places. For C, it was climbing a tree with his favourite friend, sitting high up in the branches where they could not be seen and carving little models from branches with their penknives. As they sat and watched 'the adults go by' C said they often felt no need to talk. It was just good to be there.

L went to a horse chestnut tree near her home with a friend. Again, they climbed far enough into the tree not to be seen. This was where they went to be quiet, and it was special because they knew it had probably been a private place for many people for hundreds of years.

All the children thus recognized a need within themselves to escape from the hurly-burly of day-to-day living. Yet deep within themselves they also had a sense of sacred space and hallowed ground, that sense of mystery and eternal realities referred to by Madge. The challenge within the school environment is how we are able to nurture and develop within children this openness to sacred space and hallowed ground. Crowded classrooms and schools within limited space boundaries do not make it easy for adults and children alike to have a sense of inner space. Yet Etty Hillesum in her diaries shows that inner space *can* be nurtured and developed within the most confined spaces. A primary school in Dorset set aside part of its field as a quiet area. Children and teachers planted flowers and shrubs, benches were set around it and it was there for all to use, the only condition being that silence was to be maintained and respected. The children highly value the 'sacred space' and it is often the first place they will take visitors to see. In *Children's Minds* (1976) Donaldson suggests that perhaps the challenge for adults is to place ourselves imaginatively at the child's point of view. Thus we might see our world differently and through fresh eyes.

The Whales' Song

One of the ways of relating to children's sense of story and narrative is to use the medium of story itself in exploring with them their thoughts, ideas and experiences. Using story in an open-ended and sensitive way allows children to bring their own depth and insights into the characters, the emotions, the purpose of the narrative.

The Whales' Song (Sheldon and Blythe, 1990) is a captivating tale beautifully illustrated. In it, Cathy's grandmother recalls how whales have been around long before humans and that if you listened to them, respected them, put a present in the seas for them they might call your name. This had happened to Cathy's grandmother but her uncle, much more the rationalist, describes this as utter rubbish and warns that grandmother should not be filling Cathy's head with such nonsense. Cathy, however, is entranced by her grandmother's tale and slips out one evening to lay a flower on the seas for the whales. She sits until sunset but sees or hears nothing of the whales. But she awakes during the night to hear the whales call 'Cathy, Cathy', and when she looks out of the window she sees the whales dancing in the moonlight.

In using this story with my group of children I asked them first to concentrate on it and then to try and hold in their minds whatever they responded to most about it. When we had finished I asked them to hold in their closed hands what they had responded to most and then as we went round the group in a circle to open their hands as they spoke of what had struck them or touched them most. This seemed to create an atmosphere of quiet expectation as we progressed with the story.

S said he simply loved the whole story but that the ending was magic when the whales called Cathy's name. He said that the trouble with adults and even some older children is that as they do not believe in magic anymore they end up missing the chance to relate to our animal and sea world. D thought the singing of the whales sounded very real, even though she knew what S meant about it being magical.

J said she was struck by how much Cathy believed that if she left her flower on the seas the whales would find it and would come and call her name. She called this 'Cathy's faith' and said that children often believe things that adults think are silly. This made her sad for adults as it meant they missed out on so many things.

C was very amused by the uncle who, at one point in the story, joins Cathy and her grandmother, stamps his feet and declares that whales are only good for blubber. C also found the story both 'fantastic' and 'realistic'. He saw that within it there were two perceptions of whales – one, the possibility of a relationship with humans; the other, that they are simply there for humans to kill. He felt that the grandmother wanted Cathy to tell her children the story of the whales. C became agitated at this point and said that all children should hear this story and that when they grew up they should tell it to their own children. In that way whales might become our friends, and human beings – especially children – would still be able to hear them call their names.

Earlier in my research with this group of children they had been somewhat despairing about the state of the world. They felt that we adults had let them down badly by our neglect of it. We had made the world a poor environment for both human beings and animals. L even offered the suggestion that adults should not presume to know all the answers to the world's problems and should be willing to listen to and learn from children and animals.

The Whales' Song seemed to return the group to a sense of hope, to a belief that we could rediscover the peace and harmony and balance in our world. John Westerhoff III (1980) has commented:

> Children do not fret about the past or fear the future unless they are taught to do so. They live in the joy of the present. Children live in a world of dreams and visions; they take chances and create. They find miracles believable and desirable.

Sometimes, they also throw light on areas of experience, emotion and feeling which adults have long since forgotten or failed to nurture. As Donaldson (1976) points out in *Children's Minds*:

> Some kinds of knowledge are in the light of awareness. Others are in the shadows, on the edge of the bright circle. Still others are in the darkness beyond.

Children move around and between these different worlds. Through narrative and story they can give full expression to their hopes and dreams. They can see that the world is fragile and fractured yet they have a belief that we can make it whole again, that we as human beings can be reintegrated with each other and, above all, with the animal kingdom. They wonder what the animals make of us humans. This is not to suggest that they are over-serious or lack a depth of humour. Donaldson tells us the story of the father trying to show off his 3-year-old to visiting friends:

FATHER: Stephen, are you a little boy or a little girl?
STEPHEN: I'm a little doggie.
FATHER: Come on now, Stephen. Be sensible. Are you a little boy or a little girl?
STEPHEN: Gr-rrr! Woof!

(Donaldson, 1976, p. 86)

Children are capable of learning – and do learn – much more than what we choose to tell them. In our crowded curriculum and classrooms we may need to remind ourselves of this.

The Mountains of Tibet

As the group of children settled down remarkably well on the occasions when we met and had become used to the sessions being recorded, I decided to use another story with them. This story, *The Mountains of Tibet* (Mordicai, 1993), is a children's story about the Buddhist concept of reincarnation. It begins with the death of an old man who loves flying kites. It then follows the process of reincarnation – choices about places and worlds and people are put before him. Each time choices are made and the tale progresses – a land is chosen, as are parents who appear as if they will be warm and loving. Finally in a village in the mountains of Tibet, a baby girl is born and as she grows up she becomes known as the girl who loves to fly kites.

I wondered what this group of Catholic children would make of a story rooted in a different culture and set of beliefs from their own. First, they loved the story and C welcomed the way it talked about dying and death and what happened after death. L responded in a lively fashion to the many choices faced in the 'process' of reincarnation. She thought the illustrations were 'stunning' and reflected a way of seeing the world and its peoples somehow from beyond it. She was moved by the sense of being 'out of the world' yet able to make choices about coming back into it. This was exciting. Everyone in the group felt that reincarnation was a reasonable belief, though no one wanted to come back as the opposite sex! When asked how reincarnation differed from Christian belief, L explained the word 'resurrection', but said she thought there was room for both beliefs in the world. Nor did she feel that both sets of beliefs were necessarily all that different. The whole group, through the narrative of the story *The Mountains of Tibet*, engaged with its ideas and meaning and appeared at ease with exploring what it had to say in its own right. They appeared to be captivated by the sense of mystery and excitement about reincarnation. To them it was believable and possible. It was also interesting to discover that it was through the use of this Buddhist story that the group began, for the first time, to use explicitly religious language and ideas. They began to make references to some of their work in religious education.

Encounters with lapwings

Sylvia Anthony in her book *The Child's Discovery of Death* (1940) commented:

> The child approached may close up, like a sea anemone or a wood-louse or he may display himself, like a lapwing when her nest is approached, who of course, does not display her nest but cleverly conceals it.

In one sense in our research we do not do anything that teachers do not do. We spend time with children, we listen to them, we share story and narrative with them. We invite them to take us into their 'special', 'secret' or 'sacred' places, whether these places are within themselves or in the world outside and which we adults very often fail to notice. What we have had in our research project with children which teachers today do not have enough of is *quality time*. We have had the time, space and facilities to explore with them their responses, their insights, their deep-seated feelings and emotions. That has been our privilege.

In return, we can only indicate to the world of adults what we are hearing. When C, with some passion, told me that 'adults just don't listen', it was a despairing statement of fact and not an implied criticism. He was simply frustrated that in our madly active world there appears to be little time to engage with real questions, issues and experiences. He desperately wanted to be able to do that.

The research team is constantly aware of the education

debates about curriculum, child-centred learning, standards, expectations and league tables. Interestingly, Donaldson, in *Human Minds* (1993), argues against extremes: 'Both the centred extremes in education – the child-centred and the cultural-centred have serious disadvantages.' She suggests that the cultural-centred extreme underestimates children's ingenuity, imagination and initiative. It overvalues the conveying of information. On the other hand, the child-centred extreme can overestimate the validity of children's judgements and underestimate their fitness for the role of the novice. Donaldson calls for a balance between the intellectual and the emotional. All of us adults may be in danger of losing this sense of connectedness with the inner self and the inner world. In sharing stories with children we may make the mistake of simply sharing and forget how to enter into their world. For teachers in recent years the curriculum has often become so crowded that it has marginalized the opportunities to nurture the affective in children. And who has nurtured the affective in teachers?

Yet the children in the project seem to be identifying the real significance of the spiritual, of the inner world to their lives and give the impression that adults are missing out on a great deal. However, in their wisdom they watch adults and come to their own conclusions. A group of children ('weans' in Scotland) in a very deprived part of Glasgow were moved to write about the Bosnian conflict. One wrote with profound insight and not a little warning to us adults:

> Castlemilk kills war.
> youth against Bosnia.
> weans hate conflict
> war means waste.
> Common people hate war
> weans wait for freedom
> weans watch and wait
> weans do watch
> adults walk by
> weans *do* watch adults.

Children need to have all that is *within* them nurtured and teased out in the most human of ways. Thus they would be free to echo the sentiments of T.S. Eliot in 'Little Gidding':

> We shall not cease from exploration
> And the end of exploring
> Will be to arrive where we started
> And know the place for the first time.

References

Anthony, S. (1940) *The Child's Discovery of Death*. London, Kegan Paul.

Bowker, J. (1993) *Hallowed Ground*. London, SPCK.

Donaldson, M. (1976) *Children's Minds*. Harmondsworth, Penguin.

Donaldson, M. (1993) *Human Minds*. Harmondsworth, Penguin.

Eliot, T.S. (1969) 'Little Gidding' from *Four Quartets* in *The Complete Plays and Poems of T.S. Eliot*. London, Faber and Faber.

Hillesum, E. (1984) *An Interrupted Life: The Diaries of Etty Hillesum 1941–1943*. New York, Washington Square Press.

Madge, V. (1965) *Children in Search of Meaning*. London, SCM Press.

Mordicai, G. (1993) *The Mountains of Tibet*. Bath, Barefoot Press.

Sheldon, D. and Blythe, G. (1990) *The Whales' Song*. London, Hutchinson.

Weans Do Watch: Poems by Scots Weans on the Bosnian Conflict (1995) Glasgow, Duende.

Westerhoff, J. III (1980) *Bringing up Children in the Christian Faith*. Minneapolis, Winston Press.

14 Prospects for education

Clive Erricker and Jane Erricker

An analysis of present educational policy

The research that we on the project have done so far has led us to an attitude towards the education of children which we perceive as at variance with establishment views.

The implementation of the 1988 Education Act, which introduced the National Curriculum to England and Wales, resulted in a closely prescribed school curriculum. As a consequence, children and teachers had to respond to a more content-led educational structure. This tended to marginalize areas of learning that might be considered educationally important but not significant in curriculum terms. There was an attempt to mitigate the effect of this in the Dearing Report in 1995, which reduced the amount of time children had to spend on National Curriculum subjects, and through the recent initiatives by SCAA on Education for Adult Life which addressed spiritual and moral education and education for citizenship (Tate, 1996). Nevertheless, recent though these initiatives are, it is difficult to see them as impacting on the general drive in education to identify children's learning as being important in other than National Curriculum terms.

The argument that might sustain this approach to children's education has been advanced by Callan (1988) as follows:

> [T]he temporary loss of freedom endured within the compulsory curriculum will be more than offset by the increased freedom acquired through the knowledge of various possible objects of desire which compulsion ensures.

181

This presumes that knowledge inculcated results in a greater capacity to determine the direction of one's life in relation to one's experience at a future date. The alternative argument is that unless one brings one's experiences to bear on the acquisition of knowledge at whatever point at which one is taught, then the subject matter of the teaching is not assimilated because it is not deemed relevant to the learner.

The implementation of the National Curriculum can be seen as an attempt to reduce the autonomy of children, teachers and schools and this suspicion is reinforced by suggestions that knowledge is best delivered within subject categories (Alexander *et al.*, 1992).This would result in a more prescriptive understanding of classroom teaching. Inherent in this is an apparent contradiction between children being educated according to curriculum knowledge and also being more widely versed in those aspects of education that pertain to citizenship. In other words, we diminish the autonomy of children within the school, but still expect them to be able to make mature decisions about those aspects of education that pertain to their learning beyond the confines of curriculum knowledge. This suggests that there may be a lack of coherence about the educational venture as a whole. The theoretical issue that this raises, and which educational policy has not sufficiently addressed, is that these different aspects of education demand a different attitude towards learning. If we look at the SCAA document on spiritual and moral development, Discussion Paper 3 (SCAA, 1995), we find this disparity between different forms of learning to be evident in the distinctions made between the spiritual and the moral: the spiritual is investigative and open-ended, the moral is prescriptive of behaviour. The twinning of the two approaches mirrors the problem identified in attitudes to children's learning indicated above. The issue which still confronts us is how these two different approaches can be amalgamated into a cohesive notion of educational progress.

Before we can address this we must investigate the aims underlying present educational policy in order to discover exactly what its intention is. Education does not tend to be innovative or proactive, it merely mirrors and reacts to changes and trends in society as a whole. In order to grasp both the source and the direction of movements in education we must look for the governmental influences that determine educational policy. For the most part, these influences are not educational theories, but arise from other areas of our capitalist society, such as management and economics. This is not to say that the practicalities of management or the restrictions of budgets necessarily determine policy, but the theories behind modern movements in these areas are brought to bear on education policy. If education, and the management of schools, is to be conceived of purely in business terms whereby SATs and league tables are the measures of success, equivalent to share rankings on the Stock Exchange, we cannot expect school ethos to be created whereby the school as a community can feel empowered by having established its own vision related to a sense of service to the local community and the pupils in its care. What takes the place of the latter is what we find pervasive in notions of business management: that a sense of corporate community belief and belonging can be instilled into a workforce by constructing a loyalty to 'the company' and a commitment to the success of that 'company' as measured against external criteria based on productivity and competitive achievement. This is bogus in that those concerned in this venture are not valued for themselves, but only insofar as they conform to the message they are given. In other words, diversity and individuality are not celebrated. It is also cynically unethical in that while pretending to value the individual the venture is driven only by the notion of 'business success'. It is significant that the original meaning of 'company' is *cum pane*, literally 'to break bread together', which is also the significance of eucharist and communion (*koinonia*) in a religious context. This presumes an underlying sense of belonging together on the basis of values, trust and a shared vision. If we apply this notion to schools as communities we must seek to discover in what way these qualities exist and how they are fostered. If we follow the corporate path which we have outlined above, we will arrive at a very different meaning of the word 'company' equivalent to that of *cum pane*.

The values distinction between these two meanings is revealed in the following quote from an article in the *Guardian*, 'The company we keep': 'You can't have aesthetic, moral values unless you've got economic values' (*Guardian Weekend*, 25 May 1996, p. 27). This can be seen as fundamentally wrong-headed because it implies that moral values can only be constructed within a framework established by economic goals. One might also note that the use of the word 'values' as applied to economic and moral contexts presumes the same meaning of the word in each case. This is not true. Values in an economic sense is about the value I place on something; it is devoid of any notion of relationships and community. If moral values proceed from this base, they are essentially vacuous because they have no ethical foundation. This is precisely the problem that education now faces and yet there is a great deal of rhetoric about moral values in schools.

In an article in *The Times Educational Supplement*, 'It's the way he tells them', Nicholas Tate, Chief Executive of SCAA, is quoted as saying 'We need to transmit a cultural heritage in schools which is rooted in Greece and Rome and Christianity' (8 March 1996, p. 2). In his speech at the SCAA Conference on Education for Adult Life (Tate, 1996) he stated:

> If we are to have a statement of core values, these must not be just matters for exploration, discussion and debate. As even the great liberal J.S. Mill recognised, there are some moral matters which should not be called into question. This is how it is; this is how it has been; this is how it must be.

Prior to this, Tate stated that these would be the values 'that society is authorising schools to teach on its behalf and on which schools can look to society for support when they do so'. The question is, whose society are we talking about and whose values does this 'society' represent?

We are helped in answering this question by investigating a parallel analysis of what is happening in the management of the Church of England, relating to the Turnbull Commission's report. Richard Roberts writes in the *Guardian* 'Face to Faith' column under the title 'The altar of managerialism':

> Central in the report, *Working As One Body*, is a vision of the Church as a business corporation ... The Turnbull plan is a synthesis of theology and management theory. The result, a top-down model of the Church, is not surprising ... As historian Edward Norman has argued, the Episcopal elite in the Church of England has tended to absorb and transmit the dominant ideology of its peer group, which is currently composed of senior executives and managers who increasingly control all significant sectors of society. Thus a pillar box Church will be fed with ideas from the top which come into conflict with the reality experienced at the base.
>
> (*Guardian,* 10 February 1996, p. 32)

This is precisely what is happening in education and it lies hidden in the statements of Nick Tate, the apparent transparency of which do not reveal the true meaning of the message.

In order to gain support for this notion of core values it is necessary to unite the troops against a common enemy; we are therefore introduced to the 'dragon of relativism' (Tate, 1996). Thus we are led to believe that unless we fall in behind the standard of our cultural heritage and core values we will find ourselves in chaos and our children will be subjected to the ravages of the relativist monster. This military metaphor and the moral message it advertises disguises the managerial aims which are evident in the government's desire to drive schools according to economic values.

Children are not fooled by this double-talk because they experience the effects of this policy at first hand. They are aware that tests are meant to determine their ability to achieve according to specific criteria and that the resulting qualifications or lack of them will be the basis on which they will or will not gain employment. The competitive ethos thus established constructs the parameters within which their self-esteem is measured, creates conditions of stress in their attempts to avoid failure and develops a cynicism in relation to the moral values that are promoted in schools.

An alternative approach

In this section we draw, in particular, on Gordon Wells' research in *The Meaning Makers* (1986) and the observations of Robin Usher in *Postmodernism and Education* (1994), but in a selective and adaptive manner.

The evidence, approach and conclusions of our research suggest that when listening to children's accounts of their experience and imaginative play with concepts we are forced to reconsider what it is we undertake in the business of education. A fundamental question such as 'What are schools for?' springs to mind. How do we deal with this question and what evidence is there that we should reconsider our professional role? The central issue appears to be the delivery of the curriculum. The term 'deliver' is the clue to our dilemma. If we regard listening and responding to children as central to our educational endeavour then this delivery is an aspect of, but not the sole driving force behind, our work. However, the curriculum then becomes less content-led. We should like to explicate and elaborate on this idea.

> No two children – and no two adults, for that matter – are identical. Each is unique as a result of his or her particular combination of genetic inheritance and individual experience. The recognition of this unique quality of every individual is essential, of course, as a basis for our personal dealings with them.   (Wells, 1986, p. 125)

Wells is concerned with language development. We are concerned with the development of the worldviews of children in relation to particular experiences and influences that have affected them, but there is a coincidence of aims between his research and ours. Wells states that

> performance does not depend on ability alone but on the complex interrelationship between the participants, the task and the context in which it is embedded. It is a difficult and risky business there-

fore, to draw conclusions about an individual's ability from his or her behaviour in any particular situation.   (Wells, 1986, p. 126)

Wells makes the point that the ability of children to use language in depth and complexity is not related directly to the level of intellectual functioning (p. 127). Taking this further, we may say that the level of language used tends to be related to the importance of the experience that the child is seeking to convey. Thus, if the child seeks to convey the meaning and significance of an experience that is deeply felt, he or she will resort to a form of language which meets this demand. This will most often be metaphorical in nature regardless of the child's intellectual capacity assessed by other means. To illustrate this we can refer to the way in which three of the children interviewed describe their feelings using a particular metaphorical construct.

In the first example, two boys are discussing how their family no longer feels complete because they are each missing one of their parents.

L: It's like a key that almost fits the lock but doesn't turn.
Q: What would happen if you could turn the key?
G: You'd see your family back together again.
L: It would open the door.
Q: ... And that key, can you find a way of turning it or do you think it just will never turn?
L: It will never turn.
G: It will never turn for me either.
Q: It will never turn for you?
G: No, I don't think, even if I do get another person it probably won't be like my mum.
L: No, nothing's like your mum at all.

The third child, interviewed on her own, uses a similar metaphor in order to explain her feelings about not being allowed to go to her uncle's funeral, and the way it has subsequently affected her.

S: I wish now that I had been allowed to go, cos at the

moment it feels as if I've locked up all my unhappiness and I need to get it, I need to somehow find the key and unlock myself, if you know what I mean

Q: I think that's very well put ... this key to unlocking, what is it that's got to come out? What is it that you've got to get rid of?

S: There's the reasons why he died and what I've got to try and establish is that I did have some good times and it wasn't all bad that he did die, I've got to let myself be freer to the world.

Within the constraints of a tightly prescribed curriculum and a competitive ethos there is no time or space to devote to the empowerment and affirmation of children that allows them to express themselves in this way. Without the time, and the necessary positive response from a teacher, children will not realize the value of developing the skills of metaphorical expression and of reflective thinking generally.

We are not arguing that time has to be made for a separate area of development alongside that identified in the curriculum, but rather that the curriculum should allow for conversation based on children's own experiences which can be linked to the subject matter that the curriculum provides. Children's learning and development in the context of the curriculum will be enriched by the enhanced thinking and use of language that results from this form of reflection. Furthermore, this development in children's abilities would be evidenced in assessment related to curriculum learning. In order for this to happen, space would have to be made within the existing curriculum and within schooling generally. This would necessitate education policy being less content-led, more life-skills based and a recognition of the importance of the experiences that children bring to their own learning.

This shift in the nature of learning has a theoretical base in the context of postmodern ideas. Although we do not wish to elaborate at length on this in the context of the present study, it is important to indicate, as a conclusion to our work, that there is an alternative theoretical framework within which it can be situated. Postmodernist ideas stress that knowledge is constructed according to underlying theoretical frameworks that define the character and limits of what is valuable and productive. In our present society, it is claimed that these are determined by the rules established by rationalist conceptions of knowledge wedded to capitalist notions of progress (both contained under the title of 'modernity'). The postmodern enterprise is one that seeks to undermine these 'rules', on the basis that they are political constructs which favour an elite (i.e. the interests of those in power). There is an obvious connection between these ideas and the critique of educational policy we have offered above. We are not suggesting that we replace one ideology with another but that it is important to argue for a redress of balance when it is required and that the postmodern critique is not an attempt to do more than reorient our social vision. It is a set of ideas to be found across different provinces in our contemporary world: in the arts, architecture, philosophy and the analysis of culture. Usher relates it to education in the following manner:

> Our knowledge and understanding of history and the present are relative and partial, dependent on the meanings we take and which regulate and construct our experience ... It is the consumer (the learner) rather than the producer (the educator) who is articulated as having the most power in this situation and given greater importance. (1994, p. 199)

There is no a priori reason why we should accede to this notion; however, our research has convinced us that, should we not take the thinking of children seriously in relation to their particular experiences and ideas, we do them and education a disservice, the result of which is the impoverishment of us all.

References

Alexander, R., Rose, J. and Woodhead, C. (1992) *Curriculum Organisation and Classroom Practice*. London, HMSO.

Callan, E. (1988) *Autonomy and Schooling*. Montreal, McGill-Queen's University Press.

SCAA (1995) *Spiritual and Moral Development*. Discussion Paper 3. London, SCAA.

Tate, N. (1996) Speech given at SCAA Conference 'Education for Adult Life'.

Usher, R. (1994) *Postmodernism and Education*. London, Routledge.

Wells, G. (1986) *The Meaning Makers*. Portsmouth, Hodder & Stoughton.

Name index

Subject index